Get Rich by Saying NO!

Lyle D. Victor MD, MBA

DEDICATION

To Diane, my wife and partner who helped with many of the details in producing this book and to my children Mia, Jay, Natalie and Nadine who had to listen to all my economic ruminations

CONTENTS

ACKNOWLEDGMENTS

Many thanks to   the following who listened and advised as I wrote this book. David Farbman, John Plant, Debbie Haas, Birgit Sorgenfrei, Steve Brown, Giles and Laura Teste, JD Winegarden, Dean Victor and Steve Fabick,
Special thanks to the most talented editor Lorna Gentry and my devoted sister in law Linda Agin for her spectacular graphic artistry

INTRODUCTION "GET RICH BY SAYING NO"

I woke up one day a few years ago and realized I was rich. I didn't win the lottery or fall into a fat inheritance. Like many people, I worked and saved and learned from my mistakes. Hard work and careful spending didn't make me rich, though. Instead, I got rich by saying NO. NO to ego, NO to wishful thinking, NO to the costly temptations that have lured so many other investors off the cliff.

Of course, I did say YES to things that truly mattered—things like a good education and solid profession. I graduated from medical school and became a respected pulmonary specialist, and then I went on to earn an MBA, so I could run my practice as a successful business. Those "yesses" paid off. By the time I reached my 40s, I was living well and had few financial worries. Clearly, my income, paired with wise spending and careful saving gave me a good life style. But, I wanted more than "good," more than a comfortable salary and respectable savings account. I wanted to take the next step, to become truly wealthy. To me, that meant having the money necessary to live in a great neighborhood with the best public schools; to have the freedom to do the work I love, in an environment that was both challenging and rewarding; and to have the free time and money to give back to my community. So, I set out to become rich, and I did—not by being the hardest-working doctor in my practice or the world's most skillful investor. I became truly wealthy by continuing to say NO.

That meant saying NO to living like I was independently wealthy when I was really just financially comfortable. NO to an exotic stock portfolio packed with risky investments whose potential for aggressive growth convinced many investors to dismiss their equally great (and stomach-churning) possibility of losing it all. Instead, I went after reliable, if unremarkable, returns. I also said NO to following the "herd" in 2009, when investors became convinced the sky was falling on the global marketplace and began dumping their stocks. I stayed the course, even upping my investments in index funds as prices tumbled along with the beleaguered markets. I even said NO to myself. Rather than clinging to bad ideas out of mis-directed pride, when I made an investment mis-step, I quickly owned my mistake and corrected course. Consequently, my worth continued to grow until that day when I realized that I had become truly wealthy. In essence, saying NO was my ticket to true wealth.

Over the years, I developed my skill at saying NO into a simple and effective model for growing wealth in *any* personal and economic environment. Colleagues and friends asked me to help them develop their own financial successes, and soon, I began sharing my methods with others on both a personal and professional basis. For the past 25 years, I have advised medical residents-in-training in both personal finance and wealth management, and I've brought in other advisors to the Medical Center Grand Rounds to speak to residents about investment scams. I present lectures and seminars on investing, business management, and healthcare economics, and I would wage that I've been responsible for spurring on more residents to start a Roth IRA during training than any financial advisor *anywhere*. And, I've written a book, *The Residency Handbook,* designed to give sound financial direction for senior medical students who were about to get their first paying job as a resident.

Today, I continue to spend a good deal of my time counseling other medical professionals in how to manage and grow their own wealth. In seminars and on-site classes, I teach medical students, teachers, doctors, and other professionals the fundamental ideas and practices I've developed for getting rich by saying NO. In this book, I outline and explain those same fundamentals for you. Here's a closer look at the concepts and techniques we'll cover:

- In **Chapter 1, "NO in a Nutshell,"** I'll offer a quick overview of just what we stand to gain by saying NO, and how much we can lose by saying YES to the wrong kinds of investment opportunities. Here, we'll take a closer look at some of the standard definitions for "poor," "comfortable," and "rich," and we'll check in with how income defines economic class. More importantly, we'll walk through a simple process for determining what we expect from a wealthy lifestyle, so we can arrive at a solid set of goals to work toward on our way to true wealth. Can money buy us the things that truly matter most in life? Here, we'll explore the sometimes-surprising ways that building wealth by learning to say NO can improve both the quality and extent of our future.

- In **Chapter 2, "Why You Don't Say NO: The Psychology of Investing,"** we'll explore the psychological traits frequently found among losing investors. I'll also offer an overview of the fascinating new field of *behavioral finance* which studies how psychological issues can interfere with good financial decision—making in even the most intelligent and committed investors. You'll learn how to say NO to overconfidence, loss aversion, and the illusion of control, and to recognize emotional biases including, self-attribution, mental accounting, and availability.

- In **Chapter 3, "Saying No to Elegantitis,"** we really take a close look at how wasteful spending can impact our progress toward true wealth. Here, we'll examine a wide range of common purchases and expenses that can seem reasonable, maybe even essential, but in reality, offer much less than they give back in happy returns. We'll look at the true cost of some of the most common money mis-directors, and I'll offer some techniques for training yourself to weigh the costs and benefits of even the most tempting—and wealth-draining—indulgences. We'll talk about how everyday financial decisions, such as whether to own or lease, can shape our path from financial comfort to wealth, and we'll explore the most cost-effective ways to enjoy a good life while we're still on our way to the top.

- In **Chapter 4, "Saying No to Risky Business Ventures,"** you'll learn to say no to get-rich-quick business schemes. Here, I'll be relating real-life business situations that have involved me or my close associates and family. I've changed names and other identifying facts to save all of us embarrassment (and to make sure everyone is still speaking to me), but the essence of the investment pitches I write about in this chapter is intact. In this tour of Painful Financial Learning Experiences, we'll take a close look at the particular perils of investing with friends and the dramatic downfall that can happen when investing with even the most wise and honest family members. We'll also review my top two principles for wise investment, and how to determine whether you're too old (or young) for *any* kind of risky business

- In **Chapter 5, "Saying NO to the 'Home Investment' Myth,"** takes on what may be one of the most powerful myths of common wisdom--the idea that our home is an investment. For decades, we Americans have nursed the notion that our house is some kind of super savings account with an ATM attached. We put money in and expect that money—and a hefty dividend of tax deductions and property appreciation—will be waiting safely for our withdrawal. As we learn in Chapter 5, however, we can make better financial decisions when we understand that a house is really just a consumer good, such as a car or a coffee maker. By understanding the true costs and returns of owning a family and/or vacation home, we can save thousands of dollars and the even more valuable expenditure of physical, emotional, and intellectual energy required to maintain real estate over the years.

- In **Chapter 6, "Saying NO to Investment Scams and Herd Investing,"** we take a walk on the dark side, as I outline some of the most common causes of wealth erosion and loss. Here, we'll uncover the evergreen appeal of some classic scams, such as affinity investments and "pump and dump" schemes, and how to identify them through even the most expertly crafted financial camouflage. This chapter also looks at the most powerful tools for avoiding the financial tricks we play on ourselves. Here, you'll learn how to avoid falling for popular, but losing, investment schemes that quickly flourish and die, along with your financial dreams.

- **Chapter 7, "Saying NO to High Fees and Expensive Advice,"** may offer some of the most necessary—and counter-intuitive—advice in this book. We all want to trust in our financial advisors, so we can rely on them to help support our efforts to grow our wealth. But, as I emphasize throughout this book, *you can't get rich by wasting your money,* and paying too much to a financial advisor or money manager is like setting a match to a pile of cash. Here, I'll offer an insider's look at the current rules of investing, along with the many traps that line the path toward investment success. From learning to spot a hollow sales pitch, to choosing the right funds, avoiding excessive fees, and understanding why (and how) to read a prospectus, the information you learn in this chapter will help you establish a solid relationship with a sound financial guide—and reap the rewards that relationship can bring.

- Finally, in **Chapter 8, "Knowing when to Say Yes,"** we examine the types of investment choices in which YES is your best (and most profitable) answer. We'll take a close look at specific investment techniques that can make the stock market a safe and reliably profitable place for growing wealth. This chapter offers a quick and informative "master class" in stocks, bonds, money market funds, and CDs. You'll leave this chapter understanding both the risks and rewards of interest and credit rates and the ETF. We'll also review the important complications you need to prepare for when planning an investment strategy, along with the most critical questions you must ask yourself during that process.

Despite what everyone may tell you, you don't have to work hard at investing to get rich. I wrote this book for people who *don't* want to work too hard. In fact, you don't have to even read the whole book--although I think you'll want to, because it can be quite entertaining.

This isn't just a collection of financial charts and fund descriptions. In every chapter, I've included stories about the experiences I've gathered over years of working with investors and advisors on my own, and from observing the financial mis-steps and failures of numerous friends and colleagues who at times have been blessed with more money than investment savvy. Not interested in the stories? No problem! Scan the chapter intros, skip to the charts, callouts, and "Victor's Advice" elements, and then carefully read through the summaries at the end of each chapter. Don't like financial charts and detailed explanations? Again, no problem. I've kept it simple throughout the book. My process isn't overly technical and convoluted, and my explanation of that process is equally to-the-point. Want some entertainment with your info? I've got that covered, too, with plenty of interesting stories about people and the many ways they and their advisors use—and lose— financial resources in the quest for wealth. In other words, if you're lazy, but you still want to be rich, this is the book for you. You don't have to do a lot of tedious memorization and evaluation. You just have to be willing to peel away from the herd, think for yourself, and learn to say NO. In fact, you're about to learn how to use that simple word, and the mindset on which it's based, to become truly wealthy. Because in this book, I'm going, to teach you to get rich by saying NO!

CHAPTER 1: NO IN A NUTSHELL

If you're not rich, you're not alone—there's a reason we've taken to referring to "the 1%" when talking about the wealthy. While it's safe to say that nearly all rich people are investors, not all investors are rich. In fact, out of the millions of people with money invested in the marketplace, only a fraction are wealthy enough to be considered as members of the upper class.

So, how much money does it take to be considered "rich." In 2016, a report published by the Urban Institute laid out a simple framework for defining categories of wealth in the United States.[1] Here's how they categorize the financial status of a three-person family, based on annual income:

Rich	>$350k
Upper Middle	$100K-$350K
Middle	$50k-$100K
Lower Middle	$30K-$50K
Poor	<$30K

Of course, these figures are generalizations. Where you live, your age, your health, and numerous other qualifiers can impact the lifestyle these incomes can produce. I personally don't think an income of $350,000 a year or more is essential for being—or *feeling*—rich. But, personal thresholds aside, when this report was published, only 1.8% of Americans had annual incomes high enough to earn them a place in the top-most category of this listing. That same year, Gallup reported that about *half* of all Americans had investments in the stock market.[2] If financial investments are wealth-builders, why aren't more investors rich? What's going on here?

I asked myself that same question back in 1999, when I was a highly educated, hardworking, 54-year-old business school graduate. I had a great income, invested regularly, and was careful with my spending. But I wasn't rich, and I wanted to know why. I set out to find the answer to that question and, over time, came to a somewhat surprising conclusion. Although compensation, investment, inheritance, even luck can seed wealth, growing—even maintaining--it demands that we spend wisely and avoid the investment "black holes" that suck in so many people who are trying to climb their way from "comfortable" to "rich."

One of the largest stumbling blocks along the road to created wealth is the simple inability to control the way we spend our money. Most truly rich people, I discovered, have mastered the skills for knowing when and why to say NO to wasteful spending and poor investments and it's *that* skill set that enables them to establish and continually build their financial worth.

Unlike financial titans like Warren Buffet from Berkshire-Hathaway or Amazon's Jeff Bezos, most people—including the very wealthy—aren't armed with an uncanny ability for sniffing out potentially ground-breaking entrepreneurship, invention, creativity, or other investment opportunity. And, in all honesty, you and I are unlikely to master that skill set, either. Instead, I have discovered that the most certain way to build real wealth upon the strong foundation of a good income and disciplined mindset is to do what so many *truly* rich people do: invest wisely and regularly in stable (if boring) opportunities, and learn to avoid buying into the false notion of a "good life" formed of wasteful spending on things (even ideas) that are unlikely to offer real returns. In other words, we have to learn to say NO to risky ventures, NO to grotesquely indulgent spending, NO to the empty trappings of prestige, and NO to good-meaning people (sometimes loved ones) with terrible ideas for launching a never-before-imagined business or "making a killing" in the marketplace.

Saying NO is a fundamental skill for those of us who want to be rich because saying YES is almost always more tempting. In so many situations, YES can seem like the right thing, the kind thing, the smart thing, and—let's face it—the success-affirming thing to do, even when it most clearly is *not* any of those things. YES, to your niece who needs money to start up an internet used toy business. YES, to those silver 'collectors' coins adorned with busts of the U.S. presidents that are sure to go up in value. YES, to that 1953 MG that will bring you so much pleasure (and, heck, you've earned it). Sure, you may never use that six-digit country club membership, but YES, it feels good to say you have it. YES, that $1.6 million house seems out of your price range, but it's an investment—right? I want it, and *it's an investment*! Laugh at stupid investment moves if you want, but I guarantee you that at some point in your life, you will be tempted to say YES to one.

To further complicate matters, saying YES can be a whole lot easier than building a foundation to support an unequivocal NO. Over the years, I've seen that people are more willing to close their eyes and say YES to poor financial advice than to say NO, and then do the groundwork necessary to build a sound investment strategy. Saying NO at the wrong time can be equally costly to your wealth-building program. A 2012 article for *Forbes* online tells of a Mensa investment club that did *84% worse* than the index funds as a result of members' excessive caution about moving on good investments.[3] As the article makes clear, you have to control impulsive spending, but you have to *manage* the way you invest in an ever-shifting marketplace.

That means developing and sticking with a solid investment strategy. As you'll learn in this book, with that strategy in place, knowing when and how to say NO becomes a piece of cake. You no longer have to struggle to decide whether or not to invest in people, ideas, and opportunities that come your way. You'll be better able to identify and reject problem investments, and you'll also know just how easy it is to invest wisely so that your worth continues to grow. In other words, I've written is book to help you master the Art of NO and become fluent in the proper use of YES.

What Do You Stand to Gain from Saying NO?

As I've said, I learned to say NO because living a "comfortable life" wasn't really enough for me. I wanted to become *rich*. If that desire is your main motivator as well, then we need to make sure you can define exactly what the financial states of "comfortable" and "rich" truly mean to you. Yes, the chart we saw earlier broadly categorizes financial class based on income. But, there's no magic dollar amount or professional title or possession checklist that can determine whether anyone is comfortable or rich—or happy.   Everyone has their own internal metric that tells them when their life falls into any of those categories. But, it's important that you identify the qualities and conditions that describe *your* idea of a wealthy lifestyle, so you know exactly what kind of life your financial worth must support.

I think, for example, that living comfortably is really all about living without financial worry. If my furnace goes out or my kid needs expensive dental work, I can take care of it without panicking over where the money will come from or how it will impact my other financial decisions. Wealth, on the other hand, means having the money to do what I *want* to do, when I *want* to do it. That means having a great house in the best neighborhood, traveling to fascinating places with my family, sending my kids to the best colleges, and hiring others to do the necessary but tedious and sometimes difficult work of maintaining a large and well-appointed household and its affairs.

While only you can decide where your individual "comfort" and "wealth" thresholds lie, research has revealed some general framework for the way our income affects our perceptions of life. In a 2010 study into the connections and differences between emotional well-being (how comfortable we are in our day-to-day experience of life) and life-satisfaction (how we judge our overall life situation), economist Angus

Deaton and psychologist Daniel Kahneman analyzed over 450,000 survey responses. They discovered that—up to a point—our well-being really does increase with our income. But the leveling-off point for that advance seems to occur somewhere around an income of $75,000 a year (we could bump this up to $85,000 a year in 2017). [4] Our overall life satisfaction keeps climbing, however, as income goes up, with the survey revealing no end-point to that increase. So, while the amount of day-to-day happiness money can buy may have its limits, the more we make, the better our perception of our life experience seems to become. Flying first-class or donating a sizeable amount to an important charity might not make you infinitely happier, but knowing that you're increasingly able to do so sure can.

How will wealth determine how well you live?

So, what does a "wealthy" lifestyle look like to you? To begin to form a solid idea of the financial future you want to attain, I recommend that you begin by creating a checklist of situations and conditions that describe that future. Here's one example:

- You are able to live in a neighborhood with the best schools in the state. Your property taxes are higher, but the safe, quiet, and gracious environment you live in is worth every penny (and, you save on home insurance thanks to low crime rates).
- You can afford to lease a new car every two or three years, so you can keep up with rapidly changing auto technology. You also can afford to take an Uber when you are out for the evening.
- You have outstanding health insurance which covers all illnesses without high deductibles. If you develop a medical problem that goes beyond your insurance limits, you have enough money to write a check to cover the difference.
- You can afford to hire others to do work you can't or don't want to do—housekeeping, lawn mowing, book keeping, cooking, driving, and more.

- You can afford to work on your own schedule, rather than settling for a traditional 9-5 with an hour commute each way.
- You can afford to quit the job you hate, so you can devote your working time to doing something you love.
- When you are 55, your life becomes your own—you can choose to stop work altogether or devote your time to volunteer activities that bring you satisfaction.
- You can make healthy donations to the people and causes that matter most to you, your community, and the world we all live in.

Now, create your own list of ways in which your wealth will shape your life. The items in my list are value judgments, and your list might look quite different from those in mine. But you need to know the alternatives that matter to you, so you know what lifestyle conditions and elements you expect to gain in *your* version of a wealthy life. Otherwise, you're shooting blindly at an undefined target. Knowing what you're after will help encourage you to say NO to anything that could unnecessarily get in your way.

How will wealth determine how long you live?

OK, so you want to be rich and enjoy life. But, being rich doesn't help if you are dead. Understanding how much money you need in order to be wealthy includes projecting how long you will live and, thus, how long your wealth will need to last. Predicting your longevity is an important step in planning an investment strategy. Life expectancy rates for most groups continually grow, thanks to improvements in medical technology, lifestyle choices, and environmental conditions. In the 1960s, the average life expectancy was just over 69 years old. Half a century later, that average has moved closer to 78, so most Americans can expect to live several years into their retirement.[5]

Insurance companies have invested many years and much money in the business of predicting life expectancy, and they've become pretty good at it because they *have* to be. If their actuaries go too far wrong in predicting how long their clients will live, the companies could go out of business. You needn't be a Master of Actuarial Science to take a peek into your future, though. Let me share with you some the calculations I extrapolated from a simple life expectancy calculator called "The Longevity Game," posted on the Northwestern Mutual Life Insurance Company website. [6] Though not particularly detailed or customizable, the calculator does offer a good overview of the important role health history and lifestyle choices play in an individual's predicted lifespan.

If you're a 35-year-old female, for example, here are how many years great genes and smart living can add to your expected lifespan:

HEALTH METRIC	CHANGE TO PROJECTED LIFESPAN
Normal weight	Plus, one year
No Cardiac or Vascular disease in family	Plus, two years
Normal Blood Pressure	Plus, three years
Regular exercise	Plus, three years
Eat five or more helpings of fruits and vegetables daily	Plus, three years
Use seat belts	Plus, one year
No auto accidents or violations in last three years	Plus, one year
Do not drink alcohol	Plus, one year
Do not smoke cigarettes	Plus, three years
Do not use recreational drugs	Plus, one year
Life expectancy	99 years

On the flipside, the following chart outlines how unhealthy lifestyle choices and family history can exact a toll on that long, healthy life:

HEALTH METRIC	CHANGE TO PROJECTED LIFESPAN
Very obese	Lose four years
Cardiac and vascular disease in family at young age	Lose five years
Uncontrolled High Blood Pressure	Lose three years
Sedentary life style	Lose three years
Eat fast food and few vegetables	Lose two years
Don't use seat belts	Lose one year
Drunk driving conviction in past five years	Lose six years
Five or more alcoholic drinks one or more times in a month	Lose six years
Smoke two or more packs of cigarettes a day	Lose eight years
Use recreational drugs	Lose eight years
Predicted life expectancy	37 years

You can plug in your details to get a prediction of your own longevity by visiting the site at https://www.northwesternmutual.com/learning-center/tools/the-longevity-game.

I'm not here to counsel you on healthy living, but longevity matters when it comes to building a wealthy future. Although Americans are beginning to slip behind other developed Western nations in expected lifespan, we're still living longer than ever. If the majority of your family's health history and your own lifestyle habits fall into that first chart, you're going to need a sizeable nest egg to remain wealthy through a long retirement. (If, on the other hand, you're committed to a bad diet, exercise avoidance, smoking, and the frequent use of recreational drugs, I wouldn't waste much time reading this book. Instead, you'd better get out and enjoy whatever money you have right now, while you're still vertical.)

You also should be aware that the more money you have, the longer you may live. In a study reported by the Journal of the American Medical Association (JAMA), for example, males making $100,000 a year were found to live six years longer than males making $25,000 a year. Lifestyle habits, geographic location, and access to healthcare played a role in these rates, but in general, the study found that the more money you make (the upper quintile of annual income designated in this study is at $600,000 or more), the longer you're likely to live.[7]

So, based on all of the information we've reviewed here, it would appear that we can expect to increase our day-to-day happiness with an increase in income up to about $85,0000. More money than that can bring more satisfaction with our overall life situation, just as it can help us live longer. I also think, however, that we can assume that our satisfaction with our lifestyle levels off at some point well before we hit that upper quintile income of $600,000. We each have to claim our own threshold, but for me, after a couple of hundred thousand dollars a year, neither my lifestyle nor my satisfaction is increased by more annual income. If you agree that that's a reasonable upper range, you can say with some confidence that your target income for happiness, longevity and life satisfaction should fall somewhere within a range between $85,000 and $200,000. You also now have a checklist of qualities and conditions that you expect from a wealthy life. I can't guarantee how much money you will earn or save in your lifetime. I can assure you, though, that any a well-educated, motivated, and reasonably disciplined adult can boost their chances of achieving these income numbers and lifestyle elements by learning the process and practices of saying NO to the poor investments and money wasters I'll outline in this book.

Learning the Vocabulary of NO

Just about any new skill set we learn brings with it a new vocabulary. When it comes to the skills of building wealth, you need to learn the terms and phrases people in the investment community use. That's why the final element in this book is a glossary of financial terms. I included that glossary because as you become more involved in managing your financial future, you may want a handy reference for some of the more obscure terms included in financial documents and discussions. You can look this stuff up online, but often the definitions you'll find are no less confusing than the terms themselves.

But here's some good news—you only need to know about 10 phrases and the concepts they represent in order to say NO effectively and become an outstanding investor. We'll be talking about all of these concepts in later chapters of the book, but for now, here are the ten phrases that comprise the Vocabulary of NO:

1) **Opportunity cost:** This is the most important concept in the Vocabulary of NO. In practical terms, *opportunity cost* is the total cost of the most profitable investment/expense choice minus the total cost of the choice you've made. In terms of opportunity cost's effect on results, you can think of it as the ripple effect costs of your investment choices. It's the family vacation you couldn't take because you spent $20,000 on a boat. It's the student loan your daughter could have avoided if you hadn't bought that second home. It's the investment and dividends you didn't earn on that $50,000 you loaned your brother-in-law to start his now-shuttered business. I will be calculating and discussing opportunity cost quite a bit in this book because it tends to be forgotten by people who have made a lousy investment. People who think, "It was just a few thousand dollars," after losing everything they invested in a go-nowhere venture are failing to include the money they would have made on that "few thousand dollars" had they placed it instead in a sound investment. Always remember that the

opportunity cost of a bad investment represents what you *could have* made if you had been skilled in the Art of NO.

2) **Basis Point:** A *basis point* is one hundredth of a percent, or 0.01%. Investment professionals use the term to describe differences in yields, interest rates, and so on. That 0.01% may seem like a small amount but, as we discuss later in this book, - understanding the concept of a basis point can save you thousands of dollars over time. A 1.5% fee for managing your stock mutual fund, for example, equals 150 basis points. If the fund manages over $2 billion dollars, that 150-basis point charge is substantial. At the same time, in May of 2017 Vanguard charged just 4 basis points to run their Standard and Poor's 500 (S&P 500) index fund Admiral Shares, almost *97% less* than what might be charged by other mutual funds or advisors.[8] Its frequent use and critical meaning make 'basis point' one of the most important terms to know when you are talking to investment professionals. When you use it, they'll think you know something! (We talk more about basis points in Chapter 8, "Knowing When to Say YES.")

3) **Mutual Fund**: A *mutual fund* is a collection of stocks, bonds, real estate, precious metals, or even foreign currencies purchased by a large group of individual investors and managed by a central individual or organization. The advantage of participating in these big investment pools is that individual investors can buy and sell small amounts of a fund at any time or sell all of their holdings in the fund if they need cash quickly. Mutual funds managers typically charge a fee to make decisions regarding buying and selling individual securities such as stocks and bonds. The management fee may range from 4 basis points (0.04%) in the case of a well-managed index fund (see next definition) to 125 basis points or 1.25% in the case of the average mutual fund. As of the writing of this book, some funds charge up to 2% or 200 basis points to operate a mutual fund.

4) **Index fund:** An *index fund* is a type of mutual fund in which a large group of stocks or bonds is collected and organized on the basis of the value of the company or amount of bond issue. The S&P 500 is a well-known example of a stock index fund. The larger or more valuable the individual element within the index fund, the larger that element's proportional share and impact will be within the index. Apple, for example, is the most valuable company in the world at the time of this writing and, therefore, holds the greatest proportion of the S&P 500 Index, When Apple stock goes up one percent in value, the S&P 500 index value rises faster than if FedEx stock (at, perhaps, 197th in value or market capitalization as I write this chapter) goes up one percent. There is virtually no buying and selling or trading stock or bonds in an index fund, and therefore management fees are negligible. We talk more about index funds throughout this book.

5) **Stock** or **equity**; You are a part owner in a company when you own its *stock*. The amount of stock you hold in a company represents your portion of that company's ownership. When you own shares of a company's stock your part ownership is called *equity*. It's like the equity you hold in your house; the part of the overall price that you've paid is your home equity.

6) **Dividend:** A *dividend* is the amount a company pays its stock owners out of the profits the company has made. The company has the right to raise, lower or eliminate a dividend, depending on the business climate.

7) **Bond:** A *bond* is a loan that you have made to a company or government. Whatever entity borrowed the money from you has to pay interest to you on the loan (a payment similar to a stock yield or dividend). Most importantly, the company or government can't change the amount or payment schedule of the interest it owes. Also, if the company goes bankrupt, and there is any money left over after the creditors have been paid off, bond holders get paid first before the stock holders.

8) **Yield:** The *yield* is income you earn from your investment, such as interest or dividends. Yield is usually expressed as a percent.

9) **Investing:** *Investing* is the act of placing your money in a financial security for five or more years.

10) **Saving**: *Saving* is placing your money in a security or account for less than three years because you have a plan for spending it, as in saving for a house.

There's just one other term you need to familiarize yourself with in order to effectively master the technique's I outline in this book. And that term is:

NO: *No* is defined in the dictionary as not any, negative or never. It's the opposite of yes and the most important word in an investor's vocabulary.

Victor's Advice

Investopedia offers a very simple formula to describe the very complex concept of Opportunity Cost: Opportunity Cost = Return of Most Lucrative Option - Return of Chosen Option[9]. While it's important to calculate in inflation, cost of living, and other future trends, in the end, opportunity costs can be something of an unknown without a lot of careful and complex calculation. I've used some of these calculations to find the opportunity cost of different expenses and investment choices throughout the book, but the process is too lengthy and detailed for covering in this book. There are a number of opportunity cost calculators online, however, that you can use to find the real, long-term costs of any expenditure you are considering. One example is at http://www.financialcalculator.org/personal-finance/opportunity-cost-calculator.

Are You Ready?

So, now, here's a truly important question you need to answer:

Are you really ready to do the work necessary to become rich?

As you'll see in the chapters that lie ahead, I'm not talking about the work you do at your job every day, as demanding and lucrative as that work may be. I'm talking about the much more difficult work of changing the way you think about money, spending, value, and wealth, and then changing the way you act to align with that revised thinking. In the end, this isn't a book that contains a lot of "how to" advice. Instead, it's a book that describes the things we really *can't* do if we want to make the climb from "comfortable" to "rich."

As we finish the advanced degree, land the high-paying job, and pay off the debts we may have accrued on that journey, it's easy to look around and think "Finally! I can stop worrying about money and start buying the things I want and living the lifestyle that wealthy people enjoy." But, unless we're pulling in seven figures, that's probably not true. Yes, we can live that life. But first, we have to become *truly* wealthy, and that means building an investment portfolio that can boost our net worth today, tomorrow, and in the long years that lie ahead. To do that, we need to learn how to demand a return from the money we spend. That means learning when and why to say NO to the shiny but often valueless expenses that the world constantly parades before us, even when we desperately want to say YES. That's the smart way to spend money and the surest way to get rich.

So, if you're truly ready to get rich, let's go.

CHAPTER 2 WHY YOU DON'T SAY NO; THE PSYCHOLOGY OF INVESTING

It's 1988, and you're a 35-year-old professional, just beginning as a serious investor. Your accountant and occasional business advisor invites you to invest in a new record being put together by an emerging indie-rock group. The group's never had a hit before, but your accountant feels certain that they're ready to breakthrough. He's upfront about the fact that the venture carries some risk, but goes on to assure you that if the record is successful, you could make 50 times or more on your investment. You listen to the group's previous recordings, and they sound pretty good. Your investment would be relatively modest—just $3000—and you're young and will have plenty of time to make up any losses you might sustain. Should you do it?

Answer: NO!

First, you know nothing about the recording industry or this group. For that matter, what does your accountant really know? Ten minutes of research, however, would tell you that the vast majority of new pop songs never make a penny, so you have little or no chance of picking a chart-buster. Second, if the record flops, you stand to lose every penny of your investment, and that is the most likely outcome for this investment. Again, you won't just lose some of that money, *you'll lose it all. Finally, being young doesn't make investment losses okay. Your money is just as valuable when you're 35 as it will be when you're 65—maybe even more so. If you invest that money in a small company stock index, thirty years from now it could very well be worth over $59,000. Yes, you have longer to make up losses, but those losses also grow in value of over time, representing the opportunity cost of high-risk investments at any age.*

Why are even smart people so often tempted to make stupid investments? Well, it just might be for some of the same reasons that we fall in love with the wrong people, become serial yo-yo dieters, and buy things we really can't afford. In the wake of a really bad decision, it's easy to smack our foreheads in disbelief, to question our intelligence, or to bemoan our lack of judgment and seeming inability to learn from past mistakes. Those are pretty difficult criticisms to embrace, but the real reason behind our willingness to follow a bad investment off the cliff may be even more disturbing. What if we simply are wired to believe in things that clearly are too good to be true?

It's possible that we humans actually are pre-programmed with psychological traits that get us into all sorts of bad situations, including investment trouble. When we engage in investment activities and behaviors—buying and selling stocks, for example—our brain lights up and dopamine begins to flow into our neural pathways. As we make investment decisions, our brain responds just as it would if we were an addict downing a shot of whiskey or snorting a line of cocaine. Our brains crave that dopamine rush. In fact, sweet, fat, and salty foods, even expensive cars have been shown to trigger similar effects. That's not to say that we can't control those cravings, just as we don't all fall prey to alcoholism, drug addiction, or eating disorders. But, clearly, our investment decisions aren't all based on cool and calculated reason. Instead, the very act of making those decisions activates areas of our brain in ways that we can't avoid or ignore. Our strongest tool for controlling the impulse to say "yes" to a bad investment is a solid understanding of the psychological forces that discourage us from saying NO.

Fortunately, researchers have developed a body of scientific evidence describing the psychological forces and biases that influence investor behavior. In this chapter, we explore some of the more common ways that both our shared human characteristics and our individual psychological makeup can shape our approach to investing. Whether you're prone to gambling away your money on unnecessarily risky investments, or so averse to risk that you're doomed to never achieve any real success as an investor, this chapter will help you identify, understand, and curb the psychological quirks that limit your ability to ever achieve true wealth. We'll examine problematic investment behaviors such as biases that breed overconfidence, such as self-attribution, herd behavior, and the illusion of knowledge. We'll also explore those biases of loss aversion, where our fear of making poor investment decisions results in, you guessed it, poor investment decisions. By understanding where these biases come from and how woefully wrong they can be, we'll be better prepared to reject the ideas and behaviors they spawn. In other words, in this chapter, we learn how and why we should say NO to our own negative investment behaviors.

Getting Real about Our Investment Skills

Perhaps the single most problematic psychological influence we can face as investors is a bad case of overconfidence, the almost magical belief that we are more competent or knowledgeable than we truly are--and that we're better than most other people, too.

Let's begin by considering this question: Are you an above average driver? Of course you are! In one study, as many as 93% of respondents claimed to be above average drivers.[10] We don't need scientists to tell us that's statistically impossible, nevertheless, it isn't hard for most

LYLE VICTOR

people to believe that they're "above average" with little or no evidence to support that belief. Are you an above-average parent? Are you a better-than-average giver of advice? How about listening—are you better than most? While many people will answer "yes" to those questions, the fact is that most of those answers spring from overconfidence, not factual evidence. In any area of human endeavor, unless we have some true measurement of our ability, we may not be able to comment accurately on our skill.

So, are you an above average investor? Probably not. There are millions of very smart people around the world who spend their entire day (and their professional life) immersed in the field of investment. Seventy-five percent of the top financial professionals managing mutual funds cannot beat the market in any one year, so you almost certainly won't either. If you have supernatural powers or high-level connections into the hidden corners of the business world that enable you to access information that's not available to the average investor, maybe you do have an edge over these investment "lifers." How likely is that? And then there is the time factor. Can you beat most investors, most of the time, over a long period of time? Again, that's highly unlikely to be true, even for the vast majority of investment professionals. Successfully making complex investment decisions requires vast reserves of good judgment, but it also can demand a highly tuned skill in calculation and a broad range of experiences that can take many years and countless hours of practice to develop. A belief that you can beat these odds, in and of itself, is a mark of poor judgment. A reliance on popular wisdom, vague relationships, irrelevant anchoring points, and an unwarranted belief in gut instinct are some of the more common hallmarks of investors who are doomed to lose most (or all) of what they have invested.

Don't believe me? Let's take a moment to look closer at the problem of overconfidence, and the biases of behavioral investing that feed it. By exploring some of the most common psychological miscues of investor overconfidence, we'll be better prepared to say NO to our own magical thinking and the inaccurate notions that can infect our investment decisions.

No, we don't have psychic powers.

Is your mutual fund rightly priced? Is the stock market too high to make this a good time to invest in a specific stock? Even savvy, experienced investors have to draw upon a wealth of knowledge and finely-tuned calculations to arrive at the right answers to those questions. Miscalculation and mis-calibration are common pitfalls of ill-prepared and inexperienced investors who believe that they have been "gifted" with extraordinary skills at timing the market. And *that's* an idea that offers a sure sign of overconfidence at work.

Like those who dream of beating the house in a casino, investors whose overconfidence leads them to try to time the market indices are statistically doomed to lose their money. No matter how great your math skills and gut instinct may be, if you fail to appreciate the range of prices over which a stock or bond market can vary, you may buy at too high a price or sell at the worst possible time. And many calculations that seem relatively simple may, instead, involve a wide range of variables that can be incredibly complex to sort through.

Here's a medical example: How would you calculate the number of times a heart beats in an average lifespan? On the surface, this could be a simple calculation. The human heart beats 80 times per minute, or 4800 times an hour, 115,000 times a day, 42,048,00 times a year. Using the average male life span of 77 years, we could calculate that the answer to our question would be 3.237 billion. Simple.

But, now, let's look at how many ways you can calibrate the elements of this calculation, and how those calibrations can change the answer. A female's average life span, for example, is 81 years, so that could raise the answer to 3.405 billion. And, heart rates are higher in infants and children, so taking into account the first 18 years of life, that average number of heartbeats grows by almost half a billion. But, then, heart rates typically slow when we're sleeping, so, depending on the rate of that slowdown and how many hours a day the individual sleeps, and whether the individual is a man or woman, we might need to reduce the number of lifetime heartbeats to 2.7 billion. I could go on tweaking the answer to account for hundreds of other contributing factors, but you probably can see my point. Individual circumstances and situations can change the outcome of even seemingly simple calculations by a significant amount.

I used the deliberately vague question about how many heartbeats occur in a life time as an example because many of the questions we have to ask ourselves as investors involve predicting results which may have a larger range of variability than we anticipate. And much of that variability is absolutely impossible to know in advance. Companies merge; scandals brew; cultural norms change; leaders depart (or don't). As it turns out, trying to predict the future earnings of companies can be a notoriously difficult and inaccurate process. And many of the things that drive the market over short periods of time—terrorist attacks, global innovation, natural disasters--may be unpredictable by even the most careful and seasoned analyst. That's because most people aren't born with—nor do they develop—psychic skills. And, if you're not a fortune teller, trying to predict the markets can be even less productive than forecasting next week's weather in the Midwest.

Say, for example, we want to determine what our maximum loss risk might be if we invested in the S&P (Standard and Poor) 500 index. Logically, we could look back over a period of years, assess performance, and calculate the average gains and losses over that period of time to estimate what future gains and losses we might expect. But our true gains and losses could vary greatly from those estimates, based on when within the examined period of performance we actually entered or exited the market.

Staying with this example, let's take a look at the volatile years following the Great Recession. Typically, money managers and advisors report the year-end gains and losses from funds as representative of fund performance in percentages. But assessing the risks investors faced during 2007 through 2009 based solely on those year-end reports could have resulted in a significant mis-calibration in both directions. When we review potential percent changes in our investments over even shorter periods of time, the results look much worse. In 2009, for example, the S&P index lost 38.5%, but was up 33% the next year to regain much of the loss. In reality, however, there was a 67% gain in 2009 alone, based on the difference from March of that year when it bottomed out at 666 points, and the following December, when it rose to 1115 points.

Had you made periodic investments when the market was at its low point in the first three months of 2009, when everyone was crying and bailing out of stocks, you may well have made up for losses on paper and then some. But in July of 2007, just before the Great Recession hit, the S&P had reached a high of 1552 points. Then, *just 21 months later*, in March of 2009, the S&P had dropped by a whopping 67% to hit that 666-point low. And, even though the S&P 500 showed significant 6-month losses within 2007 when it was still heading toward the financial desert of the recession, it actually gained 3.5% for the year. Further, the S&P was still losing in the first months of 2009, when it dipped by 26.7% to its low point, before beginning its recovery, even as the overall market rose by 38.5%.

We all hope that (with any luck at all) the Great Recession will be a once-in-a-lifetime financial crash. But, this example illustrates how and why the gains and losses reflected on your quarterly or monthly IRA reports can be much higher than those reflected in year-end reports. You have to have a relatively sophisticated understanding of the market and its trends to make accurate risk assessments based on *any* period of performance.

Victor's Advice

We don't have to have supernatural powers in order to build wealth. It's impossible to consistently predict the peaks and troughs of stock and bond markets. If our goal is to become rich, the best we can do is invest incrementally and regularly, remove funds when we need them, and pay minimal charges for investment advice and management fees.

No, mental shortcuts aren't the best decision-making tools.

Given the many opportunities for mis-calibration and miscalculation to trip us up as investors, we tend to look for rules of thumb upon which we can base our investment decisions. "What goes up, must go down," for example, may tell us that the market can be expected to follow long-range trends even as it dips and peaks, but we also may translate that rule of thumb to say that "the market's been doing well for a while, so we can expect it to crash soon." When the problems we want to solve are complicated and shaped by a large number of variables and information points, like investment decisions, we may apply these general rules, called *heuristics* to very specific situations so we can arrive at decisions quickly. But while heuristics may represent "intelligent guess work," they're still guesses, based on leaps of faith that we rely on because we don't know all the facts, can't analyze all the variables, and thus aren't capable of predicting the answer to a future problem based on what we know right now."[11]

Here are just some of the more common heuristics and the biases they trigger:

- *Availability bias:* Quick—which is the more common way to die, suicide or homicide? How about gunshots or drowning? While it may seem that homicides and shootings are the more common causes of death, that's because the media offers us more information about those forms of mayhem. Suicide and drowning are much more common, but get less press. For investors, the same kind of bias in available information can contribute to poor investment decisions. For example, we often buy advertised mutual funds or funds available through our workplace pension plan. But someone has to pay for those big ads in the New York Times, and that "someone" is the shareholders, and we may pay 1.3% in fees for that workplace fund, while fees for a similar T. Rowe Price fund may be 0.4%. It pays to look around rather than just buy into the readily available information that's handed to us.

- *Familiarity bias*: This bias is closely related to the Availability bias, and it involves our tendency to choose stocks from companies we're familiar with rather than from a company we aren't familiar with but that represents a better investment. Company names we remember from our youth, or even those of our current employers can seem "safe" when in reality, they're anything but. Remember, a sizeable number of Enron employees lost their retirement funds because they were tied up in the company's stock as it went bankrupt. Familiarity bias is seen almost universally throughout the free world where investors are much more heavily weighted in stocks from their own country even when the country represents a small fraction of world equity. Up to 80% of U.S. stocks, for example, are owned by U.S. investors, either directly or through pension funds. At the same time, the United States represents less than half of world equity markets, and higher growth rates and opportunity may be found in Europe and emerging markets such as India and China. Selecting investments based on familiarity can lead to poor decision-making—and outcomes.

- *Representativeness bias:* "My friend got a great car through an online auction, so I can too." "Eli Lilly has been around for a long time and its stock has always done well in the past, so I can assume it will do well in the future." "Warren Buffet got rich investing in the marketplace, so my investment advisor can make me rich, too!" These kinds of judgments, based on categorizing conditions, options, or events that share even thin similarities, represent a particularly popular form of heuristic bias at work. When we have to make a decision with only a limited amount of information, finding ways to lump the elements of that decision into a familiar representative category can give us the illusion of certainty. But think about it: even though your friend got a really good deal on her car, your friend's good outcome may be based on any number of variables that you may or may not be able to reproduce. Warren Buffet is an extraordinarily successful investor with a rare talent—one neither you nor your advisor are likely to share. While it's comforting to assume that you can leap-frog to a decision based on the outcomes of representative events or conditions, that assumption is rooted in wishful thinking and overconfidence, not careful assessment.

- *Anchoring and Adjustment bias:* Another damaging heuristic is the bias that tells us we can base decisions on a fixed point of reference that may or may not have relevance to the situation at hand. It's easy to fall pretty to this Anchoring and Adjustment bias in sales/purchase decisions. The house we want to buy is listed for several thousand dollars more than the owner expects the final sales price (and fair market value) to be. As we go through offers and counter-offers, the price lowers and we adjust our idea of the property's status as a "bargain," regardless of the property's actual value. Investors, too, can attach decisions to anchor points such as a stock price achieved at a specific point in time or from a figure generated by an automated forecasting tool. Even if that price was the result of a short-lived anomaly or a faulty forecasting tool, the investor may believe the stock is a bargain, as long as it's purchased for less than the "anchor" price.

Decisions based on heuristics can be quick to arrive at, but they also can be quite inaccurate. Even more damaging, our subconscious desire to believe that there's a quick, reliable answer to the sometimes very complex and fluid problems of investing can function under the radar as it leads us blindly astray in our investment decisions.

No, the rearview mirror isn't a good forecasting tool.

Of course, overconfidence demonstrates itself in investor behaviors unrelated to heuristics, and one prime example is the unnecessary and unproductive handwringing over a failure to predict the unpredictable. As you may remember, right after the Great Recession hit, lots of television pundits, financial analysts, and even casual investors were quick to say that they "saw it coming" and had been "warning about this" for months. Yet, how many of those warnings were actually floating around in 2006? When a person claims to have predicted something unpredictable, saying they "knew it all along!", that person typically suffers from a common side-effect of overconfidence known as *Hindsight bias*.

This is another bias we've all seen play out among investors. Almost no one actually thought the housing and financial crises of 2007-2009 would be as great as they were, but almost *everybody* thought in retrospect that they should have known, or that they had suspected the crash would happen, but failed to act on their intuition. All I can say to that is, "Yeah, right." The Great Recession represented a perfect storm of complex and colliding economic variables that may have sparked concerns among the some of the world's most experienced and keen economic and financial analysts, but the impending crash certainly slipped under the radar of the vast majority of investors.

That's the same kind of bias that leads an investor to wail that he shouldn't have invested in a company whose stock tanked after the CEO died suddenly of a heart attack. The investor claims that he "should have known the risk" because the CEO was old. The fact is that no one can predict a leader's sudden death, and no experienced investor would look back on this investment as a mistake. As I said earlier, you are not a psychic, and your investments will never ride safely on your abilities as a fortune teller. Consider it a "humble brag" when you hear anyone

33

bemoan his or her failure to predict the unpredictable, based on 20/20 hindsight.

Knowing when and how to calibrate the timing of investments isn't an innate skill; instead, it's one that takes a great deal of time and practice to hone. You are highly unlikely to have spent more time and practice . developing this skill than has Warren Buffet, or for that matter, the average investment professional. And you are equally unlikely to have been born with the psychic skills necessary to just intuit this highly specialized and extremely complex body of information. Be on the lookout for the kind of overconfident thinking that can lead you to place unfounded faith in your ability to score big in the marketplace based on your ability to predict the future or to magically intuit outcomes based on gut instinct rather than research.

No, there's no such thing as a "Master of All Knowledge."

Just as you shouldn't expect to have extraordinary powers of prediction and intuition, you also can't expect to have gathered and analyzed *all* of the data and applicable knowledge attached to *all* of your investment decisions. We live in a TMI age, and no one can master all of the available information and knowledge surrounding any business operation, model, or marketplace. When we believe that we (or those we want to invest in) fit the role of that "Master of All Knowledge," we are indulging in the kind of overconfidence that can make us vulnerable to woefully bad investment decisions.

To illustrate this point, let's look at an example of this kind of overconfidence at work from the not-so-distant past. In 1999, the internet was the place to invest and make a lot of money based on the massive growth of computer technology, and the widely held perception that the internet would revolutionize human interaction. That perception paid off as tech companies sprouted up along the west coast like kudzu in Alabama. In a matter of months, these companies would form, grow, and then be sold for millions of dollars in IPOs (initial public offerings). Lots of people made lots of money really fast. And, even though few investors actually had a deep understanding of the Internet or the innovations driving the tech world at that time, many came to believe that they did. Even worse, they assumed that dot com entrepreneurs, who had mastered obvious skills in computer and internet technologies, would be able to translate those skills into a foundation for forming and growing a successful business model.

There were multiple problems associated with this overconfidence. First, investors couldn't really figure out if the companies they bought were worth the price they were paying. The value of a stock in traditional terms includes the value of a company's facilities, equipment, and perceived future profits. But these early tech companies often were nothing more than three people working in a rented space—or a college dorm room--who didn't really produce anything other than an idea or an algorithm. These inventor/entrepreneurs and the investors who flocked to them fully believed that their business was destined to produce a profit sometime in the future, never mind that it currently wasn't producing any revenue (we talk more about how the overconfidence of herd investing in Chapter 6, Saying No to Investment Scams and Herd Investing). As stock values continued to climb, some analysts began to chafe at the lack of demonstrable profits. When the calls rang out for a new way to value an Internet company, the stock market quickly came back down to earth. Between March of 2000 and October of 2002, the NASDAQ index of small companies decreased in value by a whopping *78 percent*.

One famous example from the overconfidence-driven dot com boom and bust is Pets.com, an online pet food and products company with a sock puppet mascot that became the company's most memorable innovation. The company raised $82.5 million in a February 2000 IPO, only to liquidate a mere 268 days later.[12] Come to find out, pet owners didn't want to wait days for a Pets.com delivery of a bag of dog food they could go pick up in any number of brick-and-mortar stores for roughly the same price. Another less well-known but typical e-commerce failure involved a dot com company called eToys. Touted to be the future of children's toy selling, the company expanded quickly with an excellent marketing strategy. The company was overconfident, however. It planned inadequately for an economic downturn and failed to foresee the souring of Internet related businesses during the dot.com debacle. With the company unable to compete with major brick-and-mortar competitors such as Toys R Us and Wal Mart, eToy stock went from a high of $84.35 in October of 1999 to a price so low that, just 16 months later, the company described it to investors as "worthless."[13] While these declines unfolded rapidly, the recovery of the market was a long, slow process. It would take until 2015 for the NASDAQ to return to its March 2000 level of 5000 points. By then, tens of thousands of investors suffered the setbacks of overconfidence in the boom and bust of the dot com marketplace.

As much as we all want to assume that individuals or organizations that demonstrate great talent in one area of knowledge or performance can carry that excellence over to any endeavor they undertake, that rarely is the case. Overconfidence in pioneering entrepreneurs, disruptive business models, and slick advertising helped investors ignore the fact that great innovators don't always make great business leaders. We can keep a check on overconfidence by remembering that *none of us—* investors and entrepreneurs alike--are Masters of All Knowledge.

No, our illusions won't make us rich.

Our hunger to believe in the power of our illusions can lead us quickly down the road to overconfidence. For example, consider the psychological basis for investor overconfidence known as *the Illusion of Knowledge.* This bias involves a tendency to believe that the more information we have, the better our chances of success. Anyone who has spent any time at all doing online research knows that there's a wealth of information available on just about any topic or subject matter imaginable, but much of it is repetitive, wrong, and

36

contradictory. Investors who spend a lot of time reading internet blogs and investor newsletters get a lot of opinions and much information, almost none of which will help them achieve any more profits than they would gain by passively investing in an index fund (we talk more about these investments in Chapter 8, Knowing When to Say Yes).

And even with the most solid information, our knowledge of past events can't help us predict the future. As we learned earlier in the chapter, daily stock market changes often are a matter of chance—the company is sued for patent infringement, the CEO dies, a hacker-breach unveils damning evidence of corporate malfeasance. The illusion that we can predict future events based on our knowledge of the past is called *gambler's fallacy* for a reason. When we toss a coin, the chances of heads turning up on the first flip, the tenth flip, and the five thousandth flip remain the same--50/50. But, if we get heads five times in a row, we feel certain that our chances of getting tails on the sixth flip have increased. They haven't. Believing otherwise is nothing more than a bias of overconfidence, based on the illusion that we have a foundation of knowledge that allows us to know what we cannot know.

The *Illusion of Control* is another bias that can hurt the unwary investor. Turns out that the more involved we are in a decision, the more we think we can change an outcome. If we choose our Powerball ticket numbers, for example, rather than letting the computer generate a random sequence, we have a better chance of winning, right? No! We have the same several-million-to-one odds of winning that we have with any number. We even have the same odds of winning if we choose numbers that just won the lottery's last drawing. It's our illusion that makes buying lottery tickets fun. Investing serious money based on that kind of illusion, however, can be a fast ticket to losing it all—and that's decidedly less entertaining.

Another common illusion of overconfidence in our performance as investors stems from the inherent biases we humans have for using selective recall when it comes to remembering and interpreting our history of successes and losses. Taking personal credit for investment gains and blaming others for losses is one such bias, called the *Self-Attribution Effect.* You'll recognize this bias at work in the guy at the office gathering who's boasting that he made piles of money on his Facebook stock because he knew social media would be the next great advertising frontier, while at the same time blaming his broker for his losses on oil exploration stocks that same year.

And then there's the closely related bias of *Cognitive Dissonance,* in which the brain has two conflicting thoughts and tries to alleviate psychological stress by emphasizing the more positive or appealing one and de-emphasizing the other. For example, an investor wins big in Apple, but loses in Xerox. She feels good about choosing the winner, but stupid for choosing the loser. When she's at the cocktail party, I can tell you which investment decision she'll most feel like talking about. If you spent a long time choosing and negotiating for a new car, you're more likely to remember the reasons you're happy with that automobile than the reasons that it hasn't lived up to your expectations. Remember, this bias-based illusion isn't really a demonstration of dishonesty. It's just the way the brain works when it's under the influence of cognitive dissonance. When it comes to assessing our success in selecting investments, however, this kind of bias can create an illusion that breeds performance-killing overconfidence in our decision-making.

A similar illusory influence comes from *Confirmation bias,* which can lead us to subconsciously look for information that affirms our initial belief, even if the preponderance of evidence is to the contrary. For a good illustration of this bias at work, let's look again at the home real estate meltdown during the Great Recession. As a result of the real estate market crash, many homeowners were left holding properties that had shed thousands of dollars in value. They consistently noted only positive signs as they anxiously waited for the market to "come back," even though most evidence in the economy was decidedly negative, including ever-accelerating rates of business failures, bankruptcies, and unemployment. These owners' desperation to recover their losses clouded their vision as they ignored the real-estate-value wildfires burning around them, and instead watched the horizon for signs of change that confirmed their hopes.

As comforting as our illusions and biases are, they lead to the kind of overconfident thinking that can destroy our chances for investment success. Bear this truth in mind when an online source tells you that "you can't lose" by investing in some obscure stock for a company or venture with no marketplace presence or viable plan for growth. Or when you blame your money manager when the market is down, but take credit for choosing her when they go up again. Or when you find yourself ignoring the bad news about an investment because you desperately want to believe that you did the right thing when you originally bought in. Getting real about your investments can be an uncomfortable process, but it's always a necessary one. We can't successfully navigate the rough waters of the marketplace by clinging to a raft of illusions about our knowledge and control of investment outcomes.

Thinking Productively About Losing

Investors are in it to win. We want our portfolio to grow, our stocks to soar, and our decisions to reliably affirm the strength of our judgment. Of course, the market wouldn't exist if we all got our wish for a loss-free investment experience. As with so many areas of life, successful investing isn't about never experiencing a loss; it's about learning how to *minimize* our losses and gain investing savvy from those we experience. We've seen how overconfidence can demonstrate itself in multiple aspects of our investment behavior. In the same way, our psychological make-up and human nature predispose us to certain attitudes and ideas that govern the way we think about, manage, and experience investment losses. Understanding those behavioral "tics" can help us avoid the kinds of flawed decisions that stem from them.

At the top of the list of behavioral influences that can lead us away from making a rational, well-informed, and economically beneficial investment decisions is *Loss Aversion*. From a psychological standpoint, we humans find the possibility of a loss to be much more compelling than the equally great (or even greater) possibility of significant gain. When confronted with even a very unlikely opportunity for loss through an investment, those suffering from a strong case of loss aversion will ignore the potential upside, even when it is the much more likely outcome of the deal.

The stock market always offers the possibility of losing a substantial portion of our investment. Those losses could represent perhaps 40% or more of an index investment at the end of a year, or even 100% of a single stock investment in a particularly catastrophic year. But that's just one possibility. The market also has had periods where it has more than doubled in a relatively short period of time. For example, between 2009 and 2014, the S&P 500 increased more than 100%. Of course, let's not forget that 38.5% loss it suffered in 2008. People governed by loss aversion will remember that one-year drop much more vividly than they recall the subsequent five years of steady growth. Loss aversion is a demonstration of our determination to survive, but it also demonstrates how our fears can interfere with our ability to thrive. We can't predict what will happen in any market, but we can control our level of risk through adequate research, expert advice, and a balanced portfolio. You can't avoid all risk and still participate in investing in any meaningful way, but you can sidestep the stumbling blocks of loss avoidance by consciously reviewing and choosing the risks you're willing to take.

One particularly strong form of loss avoidance is *Regret Aversion,* in which we are as worried about making a bad decision as we are about living with the results of that decision. Regret Aversion can stymie us in making sound investment decisions because we can't bear the idea of admitting to ourselves and others that we failed, either through losing money we've invested, or by losing out by *not* investing in a great business deal. Your brother-in-law tells you that you "can't lose" by investing in his start up online business selling the new pillow he's designed that reduces snoring. You invest, not because you think he's found a snoring solution that evaded medical science all these years, or because you think he's going to beat the 5-1 odds of failing in his new business venture. You invest because you don't want the regret of missing out on a great investment. You don't want to be sitting at that Thanksgiving table next year, listening to your brother-in-law brag about all the money he's raking in, and trying to laugh with him as he reminds everyone that he "gave you a chance to make a lot of money!" Intellectually, you know his business is highly unlikely to succeed. But your Regret Aversion has you reaching for your wallet, anyway.

Again, this aspect of behavioral investing is all about our attitudes about loss. Regret Aversion isn't about the fear of losing our investment; it's about *losing out* on a particularly big win. In either case, we have to manage our attitudes about losing in order to win. And, remember this when you're envisioning that uncomfortable family dinner with your brother-in-law the "inventor": If you say NO to his request for your investment, you have a 5:1 chance of being the winner at the table who wisely refrained from joining him in his shaky venture. That's the real power of learning when and why to say NO. You can't control the outcome of any investment choice, but you certainly can take control of those choices. When you make investment decisions for the *right* reasons, you're always in a better position than when you allow emotions to dictate your choices.

Losing through Labeling

Another bias that can influence our behavior as investors is the *Disposition Effect*, demonstrated in our determination to label stocks as "winners" and "losers," and then managing those stocks based on the label we've applied. This bias demonstrates itself when we find ourselves willing to hang on to a losing asset, and then sell a winning asset to make up for our losses. I've known of investors who refused to sell their hedge fund trading currency that was down 30 percent for the year, but were willing to sell their Facebook stock, which had increased 40 percent in the same time period. Why not sell the poorly performing investment and put that money in Facebook (or some other high-performing asset)? Because, if we don't sell a losing stock, it might go back up in value and we won't have to admit to having made an investment mistake—even though we're making a huge and very obvious mistake by hanging onto a losing investment as it circles the drain.

I can speak of the Disposition Effect from direct experience. Years ago, I bought Xerox at $15.00 a share. The company had been experiencing hard times because of growing competition from Japanese and Chinese manufacturers. In fact, beyond those low-cost competitors, the company faced multiple threats to its stability, let alone potential for growth, including the emergence of scanning and fax technologies that would demand ever-greater agility from the entrenched management and hidebound practices of a one-time industry giant. I bought my stock just as the document universe was changing in fundamental ways that Xerox wasn't particularly well-positioned to master. These realities became clear to me only after I'd made my original investment in the company. When I saw the value of my stock drop rather rapidly to $7.00, I understood the systemic reasons behind the drop, but still was reluctant to admit my mistake, sell the stock, and take the loss.

Yep, I waited until it got to $4.50 a share before throwing in the towel and admitting defeat. At the same time, I sold my stock in Apple computer at quite a profit when it hit $30.00 a share, and my satisfaction with that gain helped ease the sting of my Xerox losses. Of course, Apple went up twenty times that selling price over the following decades. Had I promptly dumped Xerox as soon as I saw where it was headed (and why), and put that money into Apple, well, I would have benefited much more from my investments. But I placed more importance on the amount of money I'd sunk in Xerox than I did on the quality of that investment. Whenever you're tempted to sell a winning stock or mutual fund and hang on to a loser, remember the Disposition Effect and its costs

A bias that tends to follow right on the heels of the Disposition Effect is *Mental Accounting,* a psychological crutch in which an investor mentally separates his or her money into several different accounts, rather than viewing the portfolio as a whole. For example, suppose you had four mutual funds in your 401K, three of which went up by 12 percent, while one--your energy sector fund—fell by 8 percent. Overall, your entire retirement plan was up by 10 percent for the year. If you were under the influence of a mental accounting bias, that energy loss sector would no longer seem like part of an overall successful portfolio, but an individual, non-performing outlier among multiple other "winning" investments. As a result, your Disposition Effect bias could step to the forefront and encourage you to sell off one of those more profitable assets, so you could continue to carry the "loser" until it regained its market value. We've seen where that can lead.

Mental Accounting can cause *real* trouble, however, when investors mentally carve out a segment of their investment money for "play," meaning they can sink it into any risky investment opportunity that attracts their attention with its slim potential for high yields. Young investors are especially apt to be overconfident and become involved in high-risk ventures, thinking they are young and can make up for their losses over time. We've already touched on the high costs of missed opportunities (and we'll talk about them even further in Chapter 4, Saying No to Risky Business). But for now, you can think of "house money" in order to understand the costs of Mental Accounting. If you win $500 at the casino, you might embark on a string of very aggressive betting, figuring that if you lose, hey, it's the casino's money anyway. NO! It's YOUR money. The minute you won it, it became part of your overall financial holdings. If you lose any money from those holdings, it's a loss...*your* loss, which might include all the profits you could have made by investing the money, rather than blowing it.

At the same time, it's also important to learn to remember the long-term trajectory of investments. *Myopic Loss Aversion* is a bias that encourages investors to look at gains and losses in short intervals such as a few months or years, rather than over the long period during which most real money is made. No investment is guaranteed. Even an index fund, where you have the greatest chance of making the most money, may go down for a while after you invest. But, index funds, by their very balanced and well-managed nature, can return your patience with great rewards. A bad case of myopic loss aversion may be what prevents so many investors from even coming close to the gains made by the S&P 500 Index. When the market starts losing rapidly, they panic and sell, then fail to buy back in time to reap the great increases that result from the market's inevitable recovery.

Losing by Doing Nothing

I don't want to scare you, but the fact is that you don't actively have to buy and sell stocks in order to erode your investment returns. In fact, you can lose money on your investments simply by doing nothing. And you won't be alone if you fall into that trap. Many people hold on to their existing investments, even when their performance is screaming "Sell! Sell! Sell!", a behavioral bias known as *Inertia and Status Quo*.

A good example of this bias comes from my own family. For some time, my daughter, Natalie, avoided changing the default placement of her 401K's investment, even though the money market fund she was in earned about 2% a year. Natalie saw the stock market rising, and she was well aware that she was young and had many investing years ahead, but she felt compelled to maintain the status quo, a conservative decision of the 401K manager who merely had parked Natalie's money in the under-performing fund until she could make an investment placement decision. What if Natalie took action, switched to another fund, and then *that* investment lost money? Her aversion to loss resulting from her own investment decision had frozen her in place. Finally, Natalie came to me for advice. I put 100 percent of her investments in a stock index fund, where I knew her money had the greatest chance of earning the strongest returns. In the fifteen years since that time, Natalie has averaged 9 percent a year on her investments. Yes, her funds dropped in value during the Great Recession, but Natalie continued to invest monthly when the market was way down and then rode it right back up.

At this moment, one of the doctors I know at a local hospital suffers from this bias. She currently has an advisor who charges her a "wrap fee" to manage her retirement, costing 1.0% a year. For this fee, he will buy and sell mutual funds at no further cost. When I looked at the doctor's investments, I was surprised to see how much trading was going on in her account, but more importantly, I was shocked at how poorly her investments were doing when compared to the S&P 500 index. She had gained 6.3% for the year, while the index (which charges 0.04% in management fees) had done 11.4%. Worse, her advisor was buying mostly individual mutual funds that have an average management fee of 1.3%, ensuring that she'll continue to achieve substandard returns. Although these excessive charges clearly form a prescription for poor returns, this doctor can't bring herself to make the decision to switch to a low-cost index fund and eliminate the so-called advisor. Smart woman, not-so-smart decision, based on a bias common to behavioral investing. Like so many investors, she's afraid of making a decision that might result in a loss, so she decides to do nothing, which guarantees one.

Victor's Advice

Want to know the easiest way to make a killing? Take a regular sum from your paycheck to invest and forget about it for 20 years. Studies have shown that once people get over their inertia and start to invest, they find that getting along on a little less money per month is not a problem. Remember, once your household income climbs above about $85,000 a year, it may not make you any happier anyway.

When it comes to loss aversion's effect on saving and investing decisions, the worst form of Inertia and Status Quo bias is that of doing nothing at all. Many of us worry that we'll lose money in our investments, and so we fail to adopt a regular investment plan, thinking we'll save money on our own. Not only do bank savings accounts offer little in the way of returns (at the time of this writing, the average interest rate for a U.S. savings account is .06%, with bank money markets averaging .08%[14]), it's very easy *not* to sock money away regularly in a savings account. As a result, many who don't participate in a regular investment plan reach retirement age with no nest egg. According to a 2017 Social Security Administration Fact Sheet, almost one quarter of married couples who receive Social Security benefits and almost half of all unmarried beneficiaries rely on Social Security for 90% or more of their income. The same SSA Fact Sheet listed the current average monthly Social Security individual retiree payment at just over $1300.[15] If you don't mind living on that kind of money, then maybe you can forget about saving and investing, and just wait on those checks to start arriving. If you want something more than keeping your head above the poverty line, however, then you better get over your aversion to loss, buck the Status Quo and Inertia bias, and start saving now.

Losing by Following the Herd Off a Cliff

Humans are social animals and, as such, want to be liked and respected and included. Even though we're no longer clustering around the campfire outside our cave, few of us have totally lost the belief that going it alone can be dangerous. We may admire the noble loner, but that doesn't mean we want to be one. Biologically, instinctively, inevitably, we find comfort in being part of a group, and to cement our group bonds, we have a tendency to move with the herd. "Everyone else is doing it," may be a child's excuse, but it's one we adults could offer too, if we were being honest about what compels us to do so many of the things we do. Fashion trends, viral videos, Black Friday shopping madness—our desire to say "yes" to the herd influences just ˙ about every aspect of our life. That certainly is the case with *herd investing.*

As investors, "going along with the herd" doesn't really pay off, because the majority of investors are intermittently wrong. Savvy investment involves forming and following an investment plan. If, instead, we're just blindly "going along," occasionally we're going to follow the investment herd right over a financial cliff. A few investors see that oil prices are depressed, and oil stocks are down, so they begin buying them up. They know that those prices might still sink a bit, but their research tells them that if they buy and hold the stock, prices will tick back up, and they'll make money on their investment. Meanwhile, market watchers see that some folks have started investing in oil stocks, so they decide they'll buy some, too. They haven't done any research, they aren't following a financial advisor's advice or a carefully constructed investment plan. They're just hoping to follow someone else into a great money-making deal. When prices fall over the next six months, the herd investors panic and sell off their stock at a loss. We know that the "buy and hold" strategy has proven, time and again, to be a great way to build wealth. Nevertheless, studies have shown that the average investor "buys too high, sells too low, and is generally too quick to pull the trigger, thanks primarily to the urge to follow the market herd."[16]

We've seen the power of herd investing at work throughout history and in our lifetime. Here are just a few examples of some classic (and disastrous) episodes of herd investing—different times, different places, same results:

- **The Holland Tulip Craze:** In 1593, Holland began importing tulip bulbs from Turkey. Tulips flourished in the region, and a very few of them contracted the non-fatal mosaic virus, which produced even more spectacular and unusual blooms. By 1634, the price of tulip bulbs began rising quickly, with the rarer versions particularly in demand. People throughout Holland began speculating in the bulbs, thinking that the prices would continue their upward climb. Trading became furious, with some bulbs commanding a price equal to more than ten times the salary of the average worker at the time. People spent their life savings speculating on tulip bulbs.[17] Then, in 1637, a few people decided to sell off their bulbs and reap the profits. Those sales triggered a wave of panic selling that swept through the market. Prices collapsed and those who had been caught up in the craze lost huge sums of money. The resulting economic depression damaged the finances of everyone in the country, even those who had sold early.[18]

- **The Internet Boom:** Fast forward to 1999, when any stock that had a ".com" after its name sold like bottled water at Coachella. Didn't matter if the company represented by the stock had no profits, no assets, no product; as long as you had an *idea* for an online business, you could go public, sell stock in your business, and make a fortune. No one listened to the hold outs, who wondered how many of these companies were ever going to actually turn a profit. Buying and selling was furious, as investors flocked to speculate on what these companies "might" earn at some point down the road. And some of these companies *could* have made money, and some even did make money in the 2000s. But not before the vast majority of them bottomed out and went broke, taking their investor's money down the tubes with them. Herd investing drove people to throw their money into unformed "businesses" with no facility, no product, no experienced leadership, and no plan for actually succeeding. It seemed too good to be true—and it was.

As you can see, herd investors don't have to be completely wrong for their actions to trigger disastrous results. Yes, tulips are lovely and there undoubtedly was money to be made on importing them into 17th century Holland. But they had no unlimited intrinsic market value that made them an investment worthy of selling off the farm and tossing in your life savings, to boot. And, yes, today thousands of online businesses are reaping great profits and some of them—think Google and Facebook—have made millions for investors. But those businesses benefited from the failures of the dot com era. They found a market for their "idea," which they developed into a real product with a sustainable business model. Their investors demanded it.

For businesses, as in investing, timing is critical, but so is *planning* and having the discipline to follow a plan. That's not how it rolls in herd investing, and that's why it's such a dangerous behavior for any serious investor.

Managing Psychological Influences *and* Investment Risk

Whether the result of overconfidence or loss aversion, most of us have seen the effect of behavioral investing biases play out multiple times throughout our adult life. Yes, in life things are never as good as they seem—but neither are they as bad as we fear they will be. Investors, being a loss aversive group, tend to bail out as markets are slumping and reinvest at market highs when there is great exuberance. Those who operate in a bubble of overconfidence use mental shortcuts and artificial comparisons in order to charge ahead with investment decisions that lack any true foundation for strong, stable performance. Our psychological predispositions can play as great a role in our investment decisions as do the facts confronting us as we make them. Successful investing isn't a matter of genius. As Warren Buffet himself noted, "Once you have ordinary intelligence, what you need is the temperament to control the urges that get other people into trouble."[19]

The most effective way to avoid the pitfalls of behavioral investing is to periodically invest in solid funds and assets, and then remove money from those investments only as you need it. One problem that made the Great Recession so devastating to so many people is that they took out huge mortgages, believing that their homes would endlessly increase in value. When the real estate bubble burst and home values sank along with the job market, those same people had to pull money from their IRAs in order to pay their mortgages, further driving markets south. Instead of being able to continue to buy stocks when prices had ebbed to dramatic lows, these people were selling at great loss. When markets and stock prices are shooting up, it is extremely difficult for the average investor to stay on the sidelines. That's why learning to say NO can be an even more important skill for investors when times are euphoric than when markets fall into a slump.

 Yes, as we've seen, overconfidence can lead to financially damaging mis-calibrations in our investments. At the same time, allowing our aversion to loss, regret, and the ownership of mistakes to rule our approach to decision-making can have equally disastrous effects on our investment outcomes. But we don't have to fall prey to the psychological forces that encourage bad investment decisions. Finding and listening to sound expert advice, doing our homework, and acknowledging biases that can influence our decision-making process are the most important investment behaviors we can develop—habits that will help any investor learn to say NO to the wishful thinking, unsubstantiated beliefs, and flawed reasoning that can ruin investment returns.

CHAPTER 3 SAYING NO TO ELEGANTITIS

When a new family practitioner joined my hospital back in the late 1980s, we spoke often about the many decisions he was faced with in relocating his family from their previous home in Illinois to their new home in Bloomfield Hills, Michigan. With the school year approaching, one critical decision he and his wife had to make immediately was about where to school their children. After visiting multiple schools, he told me with great pride that they had chosen to send their kids to "Country Day," a posh private school with an excellent reputation. This doctor was earning a high salary and he could afford the $25,000 per year tuition costs. He also wanted his children to have the best chance at a successful career and lifestyle that he could offer. As an investment in his children's future, was this a wise choice?

Answer: NO!

First, Bloomfield Hills is (and was then) home to some of the best public schools in the state of Michigan. While there is evidence that private school students do better on some standardized tests, it is not clear that smaller class size and perceived increased academic rigor are more important than the higher economic status of the private school pupil or parental involvement in their Childs education. Secondly, a child's IQ is what it is. No private school, tutor, or year of study at the Sorbonne is going to change that IQ. Nor can a private school be guaranteed to improve a student's ambition and perseverance. That's what great parenting is all about and thirdly, I could find no evidence that private school attendees actually do better in life.   A private school is not an investment in a child's future. The best investment you can make in that regard is living in a great neighborhood with excellent public schools and doing everything you can to raise your children well.

As we saw in the previous chapter, there are many ways to define a life of security, comfort, and wealth. The same can be said of wasteful spending; my necessities may seem like frivolities to you, and your idea of a must-have may strike me as being totally useless. One thing I think we can all agree on, however, is that while there are a limited number of investments that offer a solid expectation of earning real returns, there are lots of opportunities for squandering money on vanity purchases and a "good life."

Collectibles, jewelry, country club memberships, exclusive private schools, even drugs, alcohol, and gambling—so often, the things we think will bring us a better, happier, fuller, and richer life instead become black holes that drain away much more in resources than they ever give back. Everything we own or do demands something of us in return. By eroding the funds we have available for investment in reliable stocks or index funds, the trappings of this spending syndrome, which I call *Elegantitis*, actually serve to make us less financially secure, less confident in our decision-making skills, and less likely to enjoy the kind of long-terms stability we want our wealth to provide.

In this chapter, we're going to take an honest, careful look at the growing epidemic of Elegantitis and its true costs, including the long-term opportunity costs of indulgences that, at best, offer only short-term rewards.

Victor's Advice

Now, I'm the first to confess that calculating opportunity costs can be a tricky business. Back in Chapter 1, I offered this *Investopedia* formula for arriving at a rough calculation of opportunity cost:

Opportunity Cost = Return of Most Lucrative Option - Return of Chosen Option[20]

As I noted, however, this formula doesn't help us determine the long-term cost or benefits of many types of purchases or lifestyle "investments" such as private school, automobiles, expensive lunches, and so on. The opportunity costs I offer throughout this chapter were the result of some long time spent in front of an excel spreadsheet— time I don't expect most people to take in the course of making daily spending decisions. So, when I advise you to consider those costs, I'm really asking you to consider 1) the basic cost of the item/experience; 2) any expected future costs (maintenance and other expenses) over a given period of time; 3) the value, payoff, or return of this item/experience over that period of time; and 4) the potential return you could have gained from, had those funds been invested in an index fund or other stable investment, returning the expected 10% each year. The most important reason that I mention opportunity costs in this book is to encourage you to *think carefully* about the way you use your money. To help with this process and in recognition of the fact that you probably don't want to spend hours wrestling with Excel spreadsheets, throughout this chapter I'll include notes that offer a list of questions you can ask yourself when considering the long-term ramifications of some relatively common expenses. These questions can help you gain a clearer picture of the benefits—and costs—that can accompany some of the most frequent symptoms of Elegantitis.

Getting a Grip on the Long-Term Health of Our Wealth

While we arrived at a target range of $85,000 to $200,000 for an annual income that supports a high level of life satisfaction and longevity, identifying a threshold for wealth is a bit more subjective. In fact, our wealth is not truly determined by our income. While different sources offer different definitions of the term, I equate wealth to net worth— the accumulated value of the things we own minus the total amount of our debt. According to this definition, your wealth can include the equity in your house (or houses), their furnishings, cars, boats, land, cash, stocks, and other financial assets. After we have added the market value of those assets and subtracted from that figure the combined amount of all of our debt, including mortgages, liens, loans, credit card debt, and so on, the remainder represents our wealth.

Where does your personal wealth place you on the spectrum of wealth across the United States? The table shown in Figure 3.1, adapted from the 2016 Federal Reserve Data by the editors of the investment tools website DQYDJ (Don't Quite Your Day Job), shows the percentiles of wealth in the United States, based on net worth.[21]

Fig. 3.1: Wealth Percentiles within United States

Wealth Percentile	Net Worth
99.90%	$43,090,281.00
99.00%	$10,374,030.10
90.00%	$1,182,390.36
80.00%	$499.263.50
70.00%	$279,594.27
60.00%	$169,550.64
50.00%	$97,225.55
40.00%	$49,132.21
30.00%	$18,753.84
20.00%	$4,789.06
10.00%	($962.66)

As you can see, at the time this data was gathered, 50% of all Americans had wealth totaling only $97,255. To put that into perspective, in 2016, the median home sale price was $327,000, with the average price at that time being $382,500.[22] The average mortgage debt at the time was $194,875, however. That means that many of those whose wealth placed them in the 50th or even the 70th percentile may have been living in a house worth a lot of money, but they were carrying a mortgage that represented a lot of debt, too. Even more relative, a net worth of $279,594 put you into the 70th percentile in 2016, which many would consider to be a pretty modest sum of money for a family of four with two kids in college and two adults closing in on retirement. In today's dollars, those whose wealth ranks them in that 70th percentile could exhaust more than their entire net worth sending two children through four years of education at a private college.[23] After that, the family could be living in poverty.

But those are the lucky folks. The situation for a large number of our citizens is much bleaker, and that's because our money has to do a lot more than just provide for our day-to-day living expenses. Every penny we spend today is a penny that we can't invest in our long-term fiscal stability. One big reason that investing has become an almost universal necessity in this country is because our once healthy and widespread system of pensions and employer-funded retirement savings has been blown up. Years ago, we could step straight out of high school and into a good-paying job that offered on-the-job-training, good wages, and a *defined benefit* pension—the employer made donations to a retirement plan and the employee retired at age 62 with a generous monthly stipend. Now, most people in the private sector have *defined contribution* pensions where we invest our own pre-tax dollars in a retirement fund and, with some luck, our employer chips in. We, however, are on the hook to decide how to invest the money.

That's a tough job for anyone, especially for someone who never wanted or planned to be an investment analyst—and who is busy building a career (or just earning money), raising a family, paying the rent and utilities, keeping a car on the road, and putting food on the table. It isn't enough to be good at our job and a good citizen, wife/mother, husband/father, son/daughter, and neighbor. We also have to be good at planning for the future, savvy about the world of investing, and vigilant about how our money functions in that world. Just in case you feel that retirement savings aren't the most important factor in assessing either our wealth or our ability to manage money, let me remind you of one critical fact: no one is truly rich if they don't have the money to support a comfortable retirement, and both of those outcomes demand a disciplined approach to spending money. Sending your kids to an elite private school may seem like a good way to help ensure that they'll go on to have a lucrative career. But if they have to shell out several thousand dollars a month for your extended senior care because your money ran out too soon, even the highest-paying job may not keep their heads above water. In essence, our retirement income and the lifestyle it provides us (and, by extension, our family) years down the road will depend on the wealth we build today.

Unfortunately, a lot of people really aren't good at managing money, and many more simply don't have enough to make saving for retirement seem like a reasonable goal. According to a report published in 2017 by the National Institute on Retirement Security, the statistics about average Americans' wealth as they prepare for retirement are sobering[24]:

- Nearly 40 million working-age households, or 45 percent, own *no* retirement account assets.
- The average working household has virtually no retirement savings.
- Taking into account their net worth, two thirds of all American families don't have enough money to meet even modest targets for retirement savings.

Even more depressing, the situation grows worse every year. According to the NIRS report, the "typical American household was further behind in retirement readiness in 2013 than in 2010 and 2007."[25]

No defined benefits, no guarantee of future income. And, let's not forget that with 2017 Social Security retiree benefits averaging less than $1400 a month, planning to live on Social Security is a recipe for unhappiness in our senior years. In this environment, just about everyone feels at risk. That means that it can be hard to determine how much wealth is enough.

Many financial experts recommend that we have retirement savings equal to 8-12 times our yearly salary. In 2015 U.S. census data placed the median U.S. household income at $56,516, and those at that median income level will need around $550,000 in retirement savings.[26] Remember, that's savings, not total wealth or net worth, which would include owned assets and monthly Social Security income. Most Americans are nowhere near that savings goal.

With the majority of Americans having a net worth of less than $100,000.00, and fewer than 10% of Americans having wealth totaling more than a million dollars, we have to admit that we have a lot less to show for our years of hard work and saving than we should. Where have all the assets gone? Yes, living costs money. Home prices and the cost of healthcare skyrocket, while wages remain flat or even flag. But, for many of us, the necessities of food, clothing, healthcare, and shelter aren't totally to blame for our lack of wealth. Instead, we have to start looking at how we spend our money, what we want to gain from those expenditures, and how we might redirect our spending in ways that will bring us more long-term satisfaction, stability, and happiness. In other words, we need to learn how our spending can make us rich.

Victor's Advice

Say YES to

- The best house in the best neighborhood
- A reliable car

- The best education (not, necessarily, the most expensive)

Clearing the Path to Wealth

The 2016 U.S. Trust Insights on Wealth and Worth offers some valuable insights on how wealthy people describe themselves.[27] Among those surveyed, 75% reported that they came from poor or middle-class families, and the majority described their family culture as being one of strong discipline and a high tolerance of failure. In addition to reporting that they were married to their first spouse, the majority also claimed that three traits drove their success: ambition, hard work and a strong family life. All of these environmental and social factors are strong drivers of success when it comes to making good decisions about spending and investing.

Of course, we can't rewrite our personal history, and certainly not all wealthy people sprang from these wholesome, and sometimes humble, backgrounds. Still, we need to understand how *our* values and the social environment *we* are creating can impact our own financial security and that of our heirs. No matter what cultural ideas and norms about spending surrounded us early in life, the way we think about and use the assets we have (inherited or otherwise) today can go far in protecting and even growing those assets over time.

That's where our investment and spending strategies come into play. We certainly can't count on scoring a fortune through a single investment choice. Yes, had we "bought stock in Google back in blahblahblah" we'd all be millionaires today. But, let's face it: counting on that kind of investment bonanza for our ongoing security is like buying lottery tickets instead of setting up a 401k. Some of the most valuable investment strategies reported by wealthy respondents in the U.S. Trust survey included long-term investing aimed at producing small gains rather than risky "big bet" rewards. This kind of investing is like baseball. Home runs are thrilling but rare; most wins are the result of consistent singles and walks that keep you rounding home base and upping your score. And that incremental progress is fine. We don't have to get rich quick, we just want to get rich. Now, let's look at some of the factors that can block us from stepping up to bat, and some simple techniques for improving our game as investors.

Spending as though Little Things Mean a Lot

When it comes to understanding where we Americans spend our money, we can draw a lot of information from data gathered and reported by the Bureau of Labor Statistics (BLS) Consumer Expenditure (CE) Survey program.[28] This Department of Labor program regularly surveys how Americans at various income levels spend the money that comes into their households. After conducting an in-depth analysis of the BLS CE data for the final quarter of 2015, *Business Insider* writer Andy Kierz and his colleague Allen Morrell determined that we Americans spend most of our money on housing, transportation, and food.[29] Of course, big discrepancies in the percentages of total income spent on these areas exist between the bottom 20% of earners, with households averaging $10,916, and the top 20%, where household income averages $177,851. But, for Americans at every income level, those "big three" expenditures drain away a sizeable portion of household income. As our household income increases, the way we spend in these areas shifts, as does the amount we spend in categories such as clothing, education, entertainment, personal insurance, and investing.

For many in that 60% range of middle-to-higher household income, however, investing still seems difficult or even out of the question entirely. We consider our day-to-day life and the expenditures that fuel it, and feel relatively certain that trimming the "fat" won't free up enough of our money to contribute meaningfully to an investment plan. But, that may not be the case. Over time, it's easy to stop really thinking about how we're spending our money, and non-essential indulgences can come to seem like nothing more than routine expenses. We don't say NO, because we aren't really even thinking YES as we lay out hard-earned cash for items and experiences that may not bring us any true pleasure, utility, or other value in return. Excessive eating out, short-lived fashion trends, questionable "collectables," vanity club memberships—it's easy to spend a big chunk of our income on auto-pilot indulgences.

So, let's look at just a few very doable spending changes that can help us take more control of our resources and get more from them in return. Even modest savings can be used to launch a first-time investment plan or boost the growth potential of the plan we're currently following. More importantly, by learning to really *think* about the way we spend our money, we are training ourselves to make the kind of smart spending decisions necessary for building meaningful wealth. That's the treatment plan for curing a bad case of Elegantitis—and, in the process, becoming rich.

Taking a Pass on Food Expenses that Eat Our Lunch

Americans love to eat, and why not? You have to eat to live, after all, and there are few essential activities that bring us more pleasure than eating and drinking. But food expenses tend to rise even above most other markers of inflation. According to the USDA, between 2012 and 2016, only housing and medical care costs rose higher than food costs for American consumers.[30] The USDA also found that almost one-third of every food dollar is spent on "eating out services."[31] The average middle and higher income families spending between 10% and 15% on food, and more than 5% of that goes to food outside of the home, which includes fast food and restaurants. So, saying NO to excessive eating out is an easy way to save money AND improve your diet.

Remember, too, that the costs of eating out also include *drinking* out. Expensive wines and micro-brews aren't the only indulgences to consider here, either. For example, my teenage daughter asked me to get her a Venti Salted Carmel Mocha at Starbucks the other day. That little indulgence cost $5.25, plus a 6% Michigan tax, for a total price of $5.57. I couldn't help but notice that we could have purchased a pound of Starbucks Espresso beans for $13, which would have given us 48 6-ounce cups of coffee at a price of just 28 cents a cup. Adding in the cost of the sugar, cocoa, vanilla, and caramel syrup, we still could have brewed her drink at home for less than 50 cents. Yes, you don't get the Starbucks experience (the trippy music, the alluring pastry collection, the impatient customers) but you save more than $5 on *every drink* by making it at home. Just three of those a week add up to a potential $780 in savings over the course of a year. And many folks buy one of those Starbucks babies every day on the way to work, meaning that they're spending over $1400 a year on a daily coffee indulgence. Those folks can save $1275 a year by making their "salted caramel whatever" coffee at home.

That may not seem like a lot of money, when it's saving the time and hassle of shopping for ingredients and using our coffee maker at home. But then, there's the opportunity cost to consider. What if we invested our savings in the Standard and Poor's 500 (S&P 500) Index at 8% return? Our 10-year opportunity cost then becomes $21,515. Invest that money for 30 years, and the opportunity cost rises to over $300,000. So, while we'll miss the social interaction at Starbucks, we can make our coffee at home and have an extra $277,000 in retirement. Which benefit brings more to our life?

I'm not trying to pick on Starbucks or the people who buy its excellent products. I use this example strictly to illustrate the potential long-range benefits to be gained by reconsidering expenditures on short-term benefits. We may think that fast food is cheaper than cooking higher-quality food at home. It isn't. That fast-food meal you snatched from the local drive-through may seem like a bargain, but in almost every case, you can cook it at home for less. Further, as our income advances, so does the price of our dining out, as we shift from shakes and shoestrings to expensive wines and truffle fries. I'm not advocating that we never dine in nice restaurants or pick up a fast meal on the fly. But we need to *think* about the way we spend on food and then make sure that we're getting our money's worth.

Victor's Advice

Here are a few questions to ask yourself when you're making decisions about dining (and drinking) out:

- How much is this likely to cost?
- When was the last time I indulged in a "food luxury" (fast food/dinner out/ gourmet coffee/a good bottle of wine)?
- How often am I allowing myself these indulgences?
- So, over a year, what might that add up to?
- What's the opportunity cost of this purchase for one year? Ten years?
- Does that expense seem reasonable to me? What amount *does* seem reasonable?
- Should I say NO?

Reconsidering Car Ownership

Where you can start to save some really big bucks is on transportation. A middle-income family (which may very well earn less than your family's current income) spends a whopping $7,767 or 17.3% of their yearly income on transportation, and typically, that means supporting two vehicles.[32] Could we get rid of one of our cars to save a bundle? I did, and here's the story.

I commute to work Tuesday, Wednesday and Thursday each week. Until last year, I leased an Explorer as my work vehicle. With the lowest mileage allotment of 10,500 miles a year, that lease cost me $378 per month. I typically put only about 8000 miles on the car, so every year Ford benefited from the 2500 unused miles for which I paid. Then, there was the auto insurance, which cost about $900 a year, and gas which ran another $900. Annual maintenance added another $200 to my costs, as did the yearly Michigan License plate, which tacked on another $200. My total annual transportation cost for that vehicle alone came to $6836.

This year, I gave up the car and used either Uber or Lyft to get to work and back. That cost me $45 a day, or $135 a week. With vacations and holidays, I travel to work only 40 weeks out of the year, so my annual commute using a car service costs $5400. That simple change saved me $1436 a year--and I don't have to drive to work! In fact, I'll save even more because I get a 1.5% rebate on the Uber/Lyft charges on my credit card, bringing my total savings to $1517 a year. That amount represents 3.58% of the BLS-reported middle-income earners wages.

Yes, you might say that looks good on paper, but what If I want to drive to the supermarket or the dry cleaners or go for a workout on the weekends? Well, for me, that's not an issue, because I do most of my errands on a bike. That solution may not work for you, but you may have other options available—a spouse's or partner's vehicle, ride-sharing or car-sharing services, local mass transit, and so on. The critical issue here is that you *think* about those options, rather than reflexively buying or leasing an automobile. Car ownership is expensive and—let's face it—it carries risks such as theft, collisions, and repairs. While it may seem that you absolutely must have your own car, the chances are that you may have much cheaper and more convenient options available to you. And all of that extra money (and time) can be used for other indulgences—vacations, nights out--with a much higher payoff in personal satisfaction. Or, you can sock the money away in investments that can bring you even greater rewards down the road. Want to be rich? Figure out a way to say NO to owning a car.

Victor's Advice

Here are a few questions to ask yourself when you're deciding whether to buy or lease a second car:

- How often do I *really* need a second vehicle?
- How/when will I use it?
- How much will it cost (gas, maintenance, lease/payment, insurance, parking)?
- What reasonable alternatives are available?
- What would those alternatives cost?
- What advantages would my second vehicle offer?
- What advantages would an alternative means of transportation offer?
- Should I say NO?

Getting Off the Clothes Horse

How about the 3% or more of yearly income which all wealth categories spend on clothing? I don't begrudge people the use of clothing as a means of personal expression, but most of the money we Americans spend on fashion should really be included under the costs of entertainment. With fashion trends shifting every season, recreational clothes shopping can become a pretty expensive way to unwind. When I committed to becoming rich, my wife and I realized we could save a sizeable amount of money each year if we ignored the fashion Ferris wheel. Instead, we shop at discount stores and buy good-quality clothes on sale.

That kind of shopping is even easier today than it was just a few decades ago. You can find outlets for well-established department stores such as Neiman Marcus (lastcall.com for men online) and Nordstrom (Nordstrom Rack or nordstromrack.com). Online sites such as Bluely (bluefly.com) and The Outnet (theoutnet.com) offer clothing by designers such as Prada, Valentino, and Gucci at as much as 75% off. And, let's not forget the number of high-end clothing discount shopping centers that have cropped up around the country over the past ten years or so. A little looking can bring you great clothing at dramatic discounts.

Of course, you can really save a lot of money if you buy good clothes in styles that you know you'll be comfortable in for years to come. You have to maintain your size, of course, but really well-made clothing can continue to look good for five, ten, even fifteen years. You don't have to toss clothes away when fashions or your waistline go through minor shifts. Instead, you can take a tip from the habits of the truly wealthy, and have your clothes updated through alteration. Recently, I invested $1000 with a good seamstress who upgraded all of my slacks and suit coats to the new trim sizes. Now, I have these great-fitting clothes that look expensive, well-made, *and* fashionable.

Whether you realize it or not, you make a choice when you purchase trendy clothing to be elegant. You want people to admire the way you look, but isn't it more admirable to be able to buy a house in a great neighborhood? And, which will bring you more personal satisfaction? An ever-changing and expensive wardrobe, or growing your wealth by learning to spend money wisely? When you're wealthy, you can choose to indulge in all the designer clothing that you want. But, you have to get there first. Remember, your goal is to become rich. Till then, keep your clothing expenses in check by developing the kind of smart buying habits that will make you look good in every season.

Victor's Advice

Here are a few questions to ask yourself about clothing purchases:

- Approximately how much do I spend in a year on clothing?
- How much of that expense goes toward a work wardrobe? Leisure and formal wear?
- How long, on average, do I keep the clothes I buy?

- Do I typically feel as though I get the full value of my clothing?
- Am I buying clothing that I need and will wear, or is this recreational shopping?
- Should I say NO?

Spending Wisely on Education

When it comes to reviewing Americans' spending habits, our investments in education shows some of the most interesting and useful data. Returning to the Bureau of Labor Statistics Consumer Expenditure data, we can see that during a time when middle-income families on average spent about 1.3% of their income on education, the wealthiest 20% of the population spent 3.8% of their income on education.[33] Of course, as income increases, a smaller percentage of it goes to the "big three" expenses of housing, education, and food, so wealthier families have more left over (and more, in general) to spend on education. Rich people know how to game the system, and in the United States, more education means both increased job security *and* a higher income. So, it isn't just a strong educational ethos that drives the wealthy to invest in their kids' education; it's also good business.

At the same time, a higher educational price tag doesn't necessarily translate to either a better education or a better income down the road. Although many parents begin sweating the details of their child's private education on the way home from the maternity ward, parents who truly want to provide the very best life for their family should, instead, focus on growing their wealth. That means saving where we can, and perhaps one of the least painful ways to save some big bucks is to send our children to a good public school.

I am not a fan of private elementary and high schools. That's because I have seen firsthand that, while carrying a hefty price tag, they don't always make a difference in an individual's ongoing academic and professional success (I except religious schools from this category, because they tend to cost less than other private schools and parents have specific reasons for enrolling their children in them). As an internship program director for a major medical research hospital in Michigan, I have recruited and taught more than 500 young doctors. Fewer than ten of them came from private schools. Getting through medical school requires many things: a lot of motivation and hard work; innate intelligence; a strong system of values—all qualities we get from our parents, not our school. In medicine, as in engineering, business, and many other high-achievement professions, you either have it or you don't. While it's true that studies have shown that graduates of elite universities and private colleges such as Harvard, Wharton, and Ross often achieve higher starting salaries, where a student went to high school can be relatively immaterial in determining later success.

That potential "wash" in value comes at a high price. According to the PrivateSchoolReview.com website, for the 2016-2017 academic year, the average private elementary school tuition was $8918; average private high school tuition that year was $13,524. Figure 3.2 shows the calculated opportunity cost for private elementary and high school. In this calculation, I've assumed that the savings achieved by sending a child to public rather than private elementary and high school is invested instead in a non-taxable account included in the S&P 500 Index (I've assumed a 10% return for these accounts; investments in taxable accounts will return about 8%, depending on your tax bracket).

Given these assumptions, at the end of 13 years, the opportunity cost for a single child's private education from kindergarten through 12th grade would be $304,437. That savings could pay for a four-year college education at an in-state university or make at least a dent in the tuition for an elite private college. Taking this opportunity cost further, if that money were socked into a pension fund for thirty years, where it could grow tax-free, the investment return would be $1,748,934.92.

Finally, while you're waving good-bye to a healthy stack of retirement savings by sending your child to private school, your taxes are paying for a public-school system that your family isn't using.

Figure 3.2: The Opportunity Costs of Private School Tuition, K-12

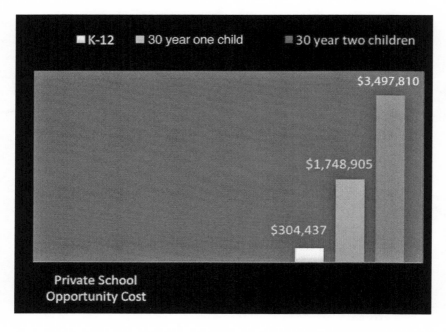

Let me stress that my belief in the value of public schooling isn't based solely on dollars and cents. Many American public schools are excellent, especially those located in good neighborhoods. Further, only you know what benefits you want your kids to gain from a private education. Higher SAT scores? Expanded curiosity? Better chance of getting into any college you or your child might choose? More confidence? Better character? Improved social skills? You'll need to do your own research to determine whether there's any evidence that the private school you're considering actually produces those benefits. Making a thoughtful, rational decision about private schooling is much more difficult than simply finding out where the richest people in your area send their kids to school. Remember, you and your parenting skills and the environment you create for your family will have a much greater impact on your child's later successes, both in school and beyond.

That's another reason why I believe that buying a home in the best neighborhood they can afford is a solid decision for anyone wanting to maximize their wealth. Along with the reduced crime and higher property values, better neighborhoods also tend to have better public schools. And, public schools tend to offer more diversity than most elite private schools. Of course, children in those elite schools spend their days among the rich and privileged—that's where Kate Middleton met Prince Harry, after all. But wealth isn't like a common cold—kids can't "catch" it from a schoolmate, any more than an elite private education can improve a child's IQ, humanity, honesty, perseverance, or intellectual stamina. Only you can decide whether or not private schooling offers real value for you and your children. My recommendation, though, is to forget that private K-12 tuition and spend the money on your home and neighborhood instead.

Victor's Advice

Here are some questions to ask yourself when considering private K-12 schools for your children:

- How much will a private school cost?
- What benefits do I hope to gain for my kids by sending them to a private school?
- Is there clear evidence (scores, statistics, college acceptance/graduation rates, etc.) that the private school I'm considering produces those benefits?
- What is the quality and reputation of our neighborhood schools?
- Does my neighborhood school system offer access to music, art, languages, and other non-STEM (Science, Technology, Engineering, Math) studies, or will I need to pursue private lessons?
- Does my neighborhood school offer a diverse and enriching social environment?

- Does my child seem to require the kind of specialized attention and tailored opportunity a private school can offer?
- Should I say NO?

Getting Real about the Value of Collections

Buying a second car, dressing like a designer's model, sending your kids to private school—these are all expensive indulgences that many in our culture view as essential investments in an elegant lifestyle. But, there's another kind of Elegantitis-linked indulgence that masquerades as an investment, and that's the habit of collecting. Whether you're talking about vintage watches, jewelry, mid-century art or furnishings, Star Wars memorabilia, or any other object of a collector's fancy, acquiring and maintaining most collections is a financial drain with little promise of gain.

Everyone thinks that they're an expert when it comes to collecting, but in truth, few of us are. Instead, we tend to get carried away in the moment, or fixated on cornering some market, and our decision-making skills take a back seat to our ego and hunger for acquisition. Yes, maybe you'll make a real killing on that antique toy truck you bought at the thrift shop in Muskegon, Michigan. Realistically, however, the chances for that are slim to non-existent. If you're going to collect anything, do it because you love the thing you're collecting and realize that the collection is very likely going to be an indulgence, not an investment.

As an example, long ago I bought two paintings that were the work of well-known artists. Fifteen years later, I put both pieces up for auction. One sold for what I paid for it, and the other didn't sell at all. Thirty-five years later, that painting's still sitting in my basement (my wife hates it). Talk about opportunity cost. I don't even want to think of what the money I put into that painting would have made over 35 years in the stock market. Even valuable artworks, like Koons sculptures or Calder mobiles, fluctuate in value, depending on shifting interests and popular demand. Further, until we become truly rich—I mean like 1% rich—we won't be buying such rare and valuable pieces. We stand virtually no chance of recouping the money we spend on lesser collectibles now.

Jewelry can be one of the biggest collectible "losers" of all. With markup rates between 100% and 300%, don't expect to regain even a fraction of your purchase price from a later resale, when appraisers may quote only the value of the stones and precious metals. I know this from the personal experience of selling my mother's collection of jewelry from the 1950s and 1960s. The $3000 emerald and gold earrings mother purchased in 1963 had a value of $1500 fifty years later. Minus that $1500, the opportunity cost of buying those earrings versus investing in the market comes to over $318,000! Yes, my mother enjoyed the earrings, but she wore them only twice a year, at a cost of about $304 each time. The real cost of the pleasure of owning those earrings went well beyond their purchase price.

Jewelry isn't the only collectible with an incredible markup and equally enormous downside. Maintenance, such as that required for classic cars, expensive watches, and even many art collections can run to thousands of dollars. Cleaning, storage, repairing, insuring—all of these expenses drag down any profit you may be planning to reap from your collectibles. When you're building your wealth, you need to put your money into solid vehicles for growth, rather than shoveling it into risky "investments" whose very stability depends on luck, personal taste, and cultural trends. Most of the stuff we collect won't maintain its value over time, let alone gain value. That's why learning to say NO to collectibles is an important skill for anyone on their way to becoming truly wealthy.

Victor's Advice

Here are important questions to ask yourself if you're considering collectibles:

- Do I know as much or more than the big "players" in this collectible marketplace? Am I willing to do the research and spend the time necessary to compete with them in finding and buying the right pieces?

- Do I have solid evidence that this collection will grow in value? Will that growth outpace that of a stable index fund?

- Do I enjoy this collection? Does it have any real purpose in my life other than its potential to grow in value?

- Should I say NO?

Reining in Your Entertainment Impulses

As we've seen, many of the active symptoms of elegantitis involve spending that truly is little more than entertainment. That's why entertainment, including hobbies, may be the most challenging area in which to save money. The BLS Consumer Expenditure data shows that even the poorest Americans spend around 5.2% of their total income on entertainment, while those in the upper 20% of income in this country spend about 5.4%.[34] These expenses include admissions to concerts and ball games, hobbies, pets, and audio equipment—the kinds of possessions and activities that make life worth living. Think about this, though; both the upper and lower 20% of income groups spend much more on entertainment than education. If we're working to grow our wealth, which seems the better way to spend our money? As you answer that question, here are just a few examples of entertainment spending that are worth a second look.

Sinking a Bundle in a Boat

As the first contestant in the Incredibly Expensive Entertainment category, let's consider pleasure boats. Michigan is second among all states in the number of registered pleasure boats—we have over a million! What makes that statistic especially interesting is that for much of the year in Michigan, the snow or rain makes it unpleasant (if not impossible) to use a boat. And boats are expensive to maintain—really expensive. That's why they say that the two happiest days in a boater's life are the day they bought their boat and the day they sold it. As J.P Morgan is reported to have said about his 200-foot yacht, the "Corsair," if you have to ask how much it costs you can't afford it." Well, you *need* to ask how much a boat will cost you over time, and whether you really *want* to afford it. Let's take a brief look at how much it costs to own a relatively modest vessel, a family speed boat.

In most markets today, you'll pay from $30,000 to $50,000 or more for a new speedboat, depending on its features (from a DVD player to radar). Don't have that kind of cash laying around? No problem, you can pay 20% as a down payment and finance the rest for 10 years at a cost of about $3055 per year. Add to that your recurring annual fees: mooring at $2000, insurance at 1.5% of total value, or $450, winter storing and shrink wrapping at $1000, registration at about $150 a year, maintenance and repairs averaging about $800, and of course, fuel costs of about $1000, depending on how much boating you do. Given depreciation and upkeep, the total absolute cost of that $30,000 boat over ten years comes to about $99,879. Of course, compared to a ten-year investment of that $30,000 in an index fund in the S&P 500, the opportunity costs of buying that boat soar to $177.673. The chart in Figure 3.3 summarizes all of the typical boat expenses —except the cost of beer, which I leave to your own calculation.

Figure 3.3: The costs of boat ownership

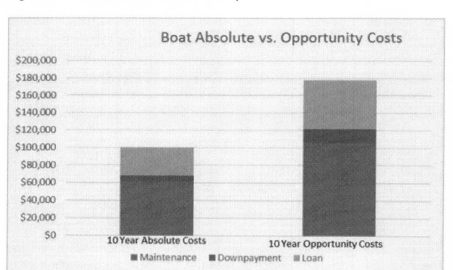

According to the U.S. Coast Guard's National Recreational Boating Survey the average powerboat or sailboat owner used their boat about 19 times in a year. That turns out to be $832 per day of use, which is probably not a very wise investment. What about a less-expensive (and labor intensive) alternative? I shopped around online and found that I could rent a pontoon boat for $300/day or $850 a week or a 21-foot power boat for $350 a day. Last summer, I took my family of four on a Muskie fishing outing for a day on Lake St. Claire. Hiring the boat and Captain (along with the five Muskies we caught) cost $400. True, I do not have a boat to putter on in my spare time or on which to entertain my friends at random moments. But the money I saved on not owing the boat for just seven years will send my daughter to a state college for four years.

Paying (More than) Your Dues

Okay, forget the boat—how about joining a country club? Sorry, but country club memberships don't offer good value for our money either. True, joining the club may bring us some prestige, but when we calculate the cost for each round of golf we might play there over a year's time, the chances of coming out ahead of our opportunity cost is pretty low. If we're just looking for entertainment, there are a lot of alternatives which can afford similar entertainment value at much less expense.

So, what are the expenses of joining a country club? Initiation fees vary dramatically, of course, from zero to $80,000, depending on the desirability and location of the club. Let's choose a local, popular club, which isn't struggling for members but at the same time, isn't overly exclusive, with an initiation fee of $25,000, payable in three installments. Yearly dues of $450 a month aren't unusual for an urban country club. Additionally, most clubs require members to spend a defined amount on food each quarter, which might come to about $1500 a year. Caddy and golf cart fees may amount to $410 for the average player (who hits the links only 16.4 times a year). Some clubs have locker fees, we'll call that $180 a year, and bag storage at, perhaps, $100 a year. There might be other funky fees, such as "hole in one insurance" to pay for a round of celebratory drinks ($35) or handicap updating costs ($40), and then there's the holiday gift fund for the staff, at another $50. Finally, there are the unpredictable expenses, such as building renovation assessments, for which you should lay aside about $300 a year. As the chart in Figure 3.4 shows, with inflation, total membership and yearly fees for a decade of membership in the club we've just outlined would come to $162,444. The 30-year opportunity cost for this decade of partial pleasure is $1,202,123. That's some pretty expensive entertainment, especially when you think about the cost of a round of golf for the average user.

Figure 3.4: The long-term costs of country club membership

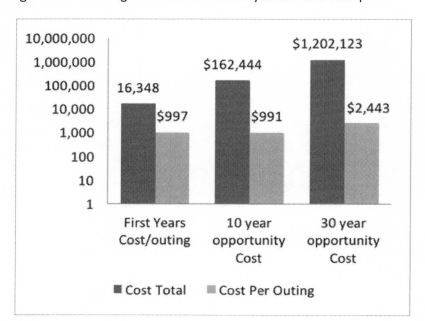

These are just some of the examples of entertainment expenses that can drain away funds which could make a real and substantial contribution to our investments. And, again, I am in no way trying to discourage anyone from enjoying their family, their leisure, and the money they've earned. Life isn't just about money, and we need to enjoy our free time. Private golf clubs have tennis and swimming for everyone in the family, and they can carry a big social and prestige factor. As we've seen, however it takes a lot of free time, money, and energy to either join a country club or own a boat, and you have to get a lot of use from either one to make both the absolute and opportunity costs worthwhile. Remember, most entertainment is *not* an investment—it's an expenditure. Travel, vacations, family outings are experiences that can be important tools for personal and family growth. But if you want to be rich, you can't forget that value matters, even when it comes to fun.

Victor's Advice

- Will that boat give back in rich life experience as much as it demands?
- Using the guidelines of our example, what yearly boat ownership costs can I expect to pay?
- Realistically, how often will I use the boat? What will each use cost?
- What will that country club membership cost?
- Am I prepared to take the occasional hit for unexpected dues or other expenses?
- How often will I use the club's benefits? How often will my family use the club's benefits? What will each use cost?
- Should I say NO?

Choosing the Best Trade-Offs

I hope you've enjoyed this quick tour of questionable consumer expenditures and their true costs. I also hope that no one reading this chapter interprets it as some sort of lifestyle judgment. I haven't written this book to either lecture or excoriate people at any income level for the purchasing decisions they make. As I noted at the chapter's opening, every individual has their own interpretation of need, desire, utility, luxury, and indulgence. That's as it should be. Our world certainly wouldn't be improved if everyone wore the same grey uniforms and drove the same type of utilitarian vehicle to the same no-frills box of a home and ate the same cheap, fat-free, low-calorie, flavorless pile of home-cooked mush for dinner. I have no trouble understanding why we want to be outside boating, shopping, swimming, and playing tennis or golf, rather than sitting at home and watching TV on a beautiful summer day. Living a bland and joyless life is not what this chapter—or saying NO--is all about.

If we want to become rich, though, we have to think about how we spend our money and what we want to get back from it. Too often, we hand over good amounts of money for things that we think we *should* want, because everyone else wants them. That other person has "that thing" and seems to be really happy as a result of having "that thing," and so if we don't want to be an unhappy loser, we need to have "that thing," too! Often, "that thing" really is worth the money, and we should buy it or do it or experience it. But, that certainly isn't always the case. And, if our goal is to get rich, to develop a foundation of wealth large enough to enable us to engage with the world the way *we* want to engage with it, to have the environment and experiences that truly contribute to the life we want to lead, mindlessly splashing out money for things that don't give back real value is the worst possible decision we can make. Mindless recreational spending can become a wealth-killing habit.

As I hope this chapter has demonstrated, if we spend just a moment to ask ourselves critical questions about our expenditures, we're giving ourselves the opportunity to make a better choice—and to develop spending habits that will help us grow and maintain our wealth. Those habits begin with learning to say NO to unexamined spending on low-return indulgences.

Victor's Advice

Finally, here are some questions you should ask yourself whenever you're weighing the costs and returns of a major expense:

- Do I really want or need this?
- How will this improve my life?

- How much will this cost—both in immediate expense and in opportunity costs?
- Are there alternative ways for using this money that will bring me greater value?
- Do I want to say NO to spending this money, so I can say YES to investing it?

Chapter 4: Saying No to Risky Businesses and Loans

Your wife's brother Scott, a university professor with a PhD in engineering, has received a series of patents for a new two-wheel personal transportation device, the PT Board, which is collapsible, portable, and has a long battery life that makes it ideal for commuting. Scott also recently completed his MBA, and he's now ready to go into business manufacturing and selling the devices. Several investors already have put up about $300,000, but Scott needs another $200,000 and is willing to sell you one percent of the business for $30, 000. Scott's prospectus projects a 30% per year return on investment under ideal business conditions. Scott, an extremely accommodating person who is almost universally well-liked, intends to run the business himself. You are confident that the invention is unique and has great potential. Given Scott's affable personality and business degree, you also are confident that this will be a great investment. Your wife has mentioned several times that your investment also would help her brother on his way to great success. You both have been dreaming of buying a vacation home, and the money you might earn from this investment could make that happen.

The Question: Should you invest?

*The Answer: **No!***

Here's why:

- *In the best of circumstances, 80% of all new businesses fail, so you begin with only a 20% chance of investment success.*

- *While Scott may be both a fine person and a successful inventor, those qualities aren't adequate preparation for running a business. Neither is an MBA backed with no front-line business experience. Would you hire a doctor who is a really nice guy with a degree from an outstanding medical school to run your drug store? Being well-liked and accommodating is a great thing for a brother-in-law or friend, but those characteristics aren't at the top of the "essentials" list for those trying to launch a start-up.*

- *The personal transport device business is very competitive and the market for these products, while potentially substantial, remains limited. What do you (or Scott, for that matter) know about competing in this business?*

- *He's your brother-in-law! You'll be seeing him at every family function for years to come. Do you really want to have to control your anger at each of those events if Scott's "revolutionary" transportation device goes nowhere?*

Whether we realize it or not, all of us are marks. Know what that means? A *mark* is a person who is targeted for being taken advantage of, manipulated, or swindled. All of us, at one time or another, will fall into that category, and often, the people who target us are loved ones, business associates, or friends. You see, it isn't just the Nigerian prince whose name popped up in our email inbox who might try to take our money and disappear with it. Even well-meaning, sincere people who care about us can encourage us to invest in "sure things" that are anything but—the new restaurant, the online start-up venture, the exciting new invention that's certain to be the next big thing. When you're a young professional with a bit of extra income to spend, lots of people will want to give you a chance to put some of that money their way or in a business or venture in which they've already invested. No matter how exciting or innovative or ripe for rewards these investment ideas may seem, though, your only wise choice is to say NO.

As we learned back in chapter 2, new businesses and ventures have an abysmally small chance of succeeding. That means your money has a very great chance of evaporating if you invest it in someone else's unrealized dream. It's true that young investors typically can take on more risk, because they have more years in which to recover their losses. But, if you lose everything in an investment, you aren't ever going to earn that money back. The harsh truth is that investing in new businesses is a high-risk activity at any age. Instead, wise investors—young and old alike—know that they need to invest in their own dreams. If your dream is to become rich, you need to begin making sound and solid investments early on, so the money you earn today has an opportunity to multiply over time. Further, you have to become comfortable saying NO to risky business investments, so that your money is working for *you*.

When someone you love or admire approaches you with an investment idea or asks for a short-term loan, your first response may be to smile and reach for your wallet. When those investments or businesses go bad, however, as they almost always do, it can be pretty difficult to keep smiling. And, believe me, I speak from experience. In this chapter, I share with you a few real-life stories of investments between friends, family, and colleagues that went south—often, after inflicting ugly and long-lasting damage to both the finances and goodwill of the individuals involved.

Because I know how difficult it can be to turn down a potentially hot, but horribly risky, investment, I've devoted this chapter to stories that illustrate both the appeal of risky business investments and the toll they can take. Here, we to take a closer look at the dynamics of investing in new business ventures, and we explore answers to some difficult questions we'll face when those investments involve people close to us. Shouldn't we have faith and trust in our family and friends? How can we make the most difficult decisions about how to invest our money? What's the most reliable method for calculating the true costs of any investment? Is it ever smart to turn over our money to a new business venture, or to simply give money as a loan to family or friends? Yes, it can be difficult to say NO to people and ideas that appeal to our emotions, but it *can* be done—and it's an essential skill for anyone committed to building wealth.

To help you use and build that skill quickly and effectively, I've organized this chapter around some important principles of investing. I developed these principles and used them successfully to steer clear of the quicksand of risky investments. They helped make me rich, they've helped many others grow rich, and, as this chapter explains, they can help you become rich, too. By leveraging these powerful tools and other ideas outlined in this chapter, you can learn how to identify and say NO to high-risk, low-potential business investments, no matter who (or what) is asking you to say YES.

Victor's Advice

Remember that 80% of all new businesses fail.

Victor's Principle Number One: Invest in Yourself

Whenever I'm approached by someone with a "fabulous" investment offer, my first thought is, "Thanks, but I can lose my own money, I don't need you to do it for me!" I don't mean to sound snarky, but I've learned over a lifetime of painful experience that you almost *always* lose money that you invest in someone else's newly hatched dream. Yes, dreams do come true—but not all that often. That makes investing in them way too risky for anyone committed to using their money to build real wealth. Ask anyone who's launched a business or sold an idea, and they'll probably be happy to tell you about the many financial nightmares they had to live through in the process. Well, I didn't earn my money in order to help someone else launch their dream of success. I want my money to make *me* rich. That's *my* dream.

What about you? Would you like to invest in this book for a share of my royalties? I'm a respected doctor and financial advisor, with a publishing history, a strong professional network, and an active speaking and consulting practice and platform. Wouldn't you like to profit from my hard work and well-established marketplace?

Your answer, of course, should be NO. Even if this book turns out to be an Amazon best seller, it's highly unlikely that you'd see any return on your investment. According to a 2016 blog post by Steven Piersanti, President of Berrett-Koehler Publishers, while the number of books being published has exploded, sales have not, with the average nonfiction book selling less than 2000 copies in its lifetime.[35] As a result of this saturated marketplace and the rapid growth of alternative means of publishing and distributing written works, the world of publishing is in turmoil. Advances can be low, with royalties shrinking right along with discounted sales prices.

In fact, I'm not writing this book to rake in royalties (though, I'll certainly accept any that come my way). No, I'm writing it because, as my father once said, "If you write a book, people think you know something," and that can offer a world of opportunities for financial gain. I've written four medical books, none of which ever sold more than 1000 copies. Because of those books, though, I am paid a handsome fee to be an expert witness in court cases, and I've had a number of valuable academic appointments. I may not make much money on book sales, but lectures, appearances, and a web site with paid advertising are just some of the ways I could profit from this investment. But a reasonable return to you on your royalty-based investment? Not likely.

I stepped you through that process for a few reasons. First, it illustrates the importance of understanding the marketplace and industry related to any investment you're considering. And, this example also shows how little we can know about the goals, motivations, and capabilities driving the entrepreneurs looking for our investment. What we *do* know is that most new business ventures, products, and processes produce no profits at all, or only enough profits to repay the person or company who brought them forward. If you want to be a philanthropist, donate away. But if you want to be rich, you have to invest *your* money in advancing *your* best interests—not in carrying the risks of someone else's vision quest.

That reality, cold as it is, forms one of the essential principles of my investment philosophy, principles that I share with all of the students and professionals I counsel on investment strategies:

Victor's Principle #1: Invest in yourself.

As simple as that principle may sound, it can be damned hard to follow. I know that from my own experience and from those of the many individuals I've helped as they struggled to manage and grow their wealth. Back in Chapter 2 we talked about emotional investing, about the hidden power of sometimes totally illogical ideas, and about how our desire to see things as we want them to be can blind us to how things really are. Emotional investing is the beating heart of most risky business ventures. So, yes, I understand the powerful pull of risky investments. If risky ventures weren't very compelling to a lot of people, we wouldn't be talking about them now. I've also seen the power of these ideas play out time and again, among new investors, old investors, and people who in other respects have mastered the art of unemotional decision-making. That power lies in a few often hard-to-discern qualities.

First, risky business ideas and ventures often seem to be disruptive forces, destined to change common practice or wisdom. That's what makes them "new," after all. Unfortunately, it's not uncommon for these revolutionary developments to, in fact, be nothing more than a variation on ideas that have already been tested and abandoned by other innovators in other industries or markets—or even for them to be too far ahead of their time to really take off.

Secondly, sometimes we are compelled to invest in the people behind a business venture, no matter how risky that venture may seem. When a family member, trusted friend, or respected colleague approaches us with an investment idea, we want to believe in it. Some of that comes from altruism. "Wouldn't it be great to give Uncle Billy a hand-up on his way to the top?" "I've always admired Ms. Gresham, and now she's turning to me for support." "It's not much money, and I can afford to risk it." On the other hand, we're also afraid of missing out. "How great would it be to get in on the ground-floor of something that changes everything? What if this long shot succeeds and I lose out because I was too scared or narrow-minded to recognize a visionary idea?"

You can find a million reasons to justify a poor investment, but you'll still lose your money. You have to be strong to say NO when a risky venture comes calling. You'll need that skill to stay true to Investment Principle #1, by investing your money in you. Now, let's examine just how these bad investments can look so good, and how you can teach yourself to identify the risks they involve.

Victor's Advice

You're almost always better off investing in stable, well-managed funds than in private businesses.

The Particular Perils of Investing with Friends

As much as we love our friends, investing our money with them can be a one-way ticket to loss—of both our money and our friendship. Even if you're eventually able to recover most of your investment, you are almost certain to earn less than you would have had you invested the money in a more stable and profitable asset. Here's the story of just one such "friendly" investment-gone-wrong from my own past.

In 1991, I was approached by my tennis buddy "Morris," with an investment idea that sounded pretty good. During the 1970s and 80s, Morris had gained some real success as a house flipper, buying up houses in working class neighborhoods, making modest repairs, then selling them at a big profit. But the real estate crash of 1990 had hit Morris hard, pushing him into bankruptcy just as he reached his 60th birthday. Just a year later, however, both the housing market and Morris had managed a modest comeback, and now he was ready to get back into business, by launching a major house-flipping enterprise.

Several of his family and friends had bought into his business, to a tune of about $300,000, but Morris felt that he needed at least half a million to really get the business going. For an investment of just $10,000, Morris promised that I would get a 25% per year return on my money. The stock market had lost 6.6% in its most recent year and intermediate government bonds, which are risk free and backed by the US government, had a current yield of 8.0%. Was I interested?

I truly liked Morris, and I was thrilled that he was back on his feet and ready to get back into business. I also knew that he'd had a lot of success in this business. While the idea had some immediate appeal to me, after some careful thought, I turned Morris down. I asked myself these questions in order to make that decision:

1. **Does this business stand a real chance of beating the odds?**
   From a statistical standpoint, the odds were against this proposal. In my heart, I wanted to help Morris and to believe

that his offer might lead to real investment payoffs. But intellectually, I knew that the statistics were against him. As Figure 4.1 shows, the odds of any new business being successful over a period of several years are only 1 in 5. As you can see, 30% of new businesses are gone in three years, 50% disappear within five years, and only 20% will make it as long as 20 years. So, is the "promise" of a 25% return worth the risk of investing in a venture with an 80% probability of failing in the long-term? The answer is NO.

2. **Am I in any position to analyze this business and the primary factors that will contribute to its long-term success or failure?** I'd purchased my own home, but that was the extent of my experience in real estate. I knew nothing about house-flipping, real estate finance, sales trends, and the overall long-term projections for the marketplace. I did know, however, that real estate was a boom and bust business for the people doing it every day, so I thought there was a very real likelihood that Morris's business (and my investment) would go bust.

3. **Does the person offering the investment opportunity have both a winning idea and the entrepreneurial skills to carry it off?** As much as I liked him, I had to ask myself if Morris had what it took to make a success of this new venture. My honest answer was NO. He was already past 60, so he didn't have the energy and stamina of a youth to help him withstand the long hours, hard work, and stress of getting a new business off the ground. And his idea wasn't earth-shakenly new. He'd be competing in a crowded marketplace. Finally, I knew he'd failed in this business once before. Everyone's back-story is different, but you have to know—and carefully investigate—that back-story before you invest your money in someone's ability as an entrepreneur. Here are the most important traits you should look for in a person whose new business you're considering backing:

- They have a vision of their product or service that others lack
- They're self-confident

- They see failure as opportunity and learn from their mistakes
- They're extroverted
- They're not afraid to work hard and take risks
- They know how to manage money
- They know their customers
- They know how to build teams and negotiate
- They are young
- They value their reputation

4. **Is there a safer and/or more lucrative way to invest in this market?** If you're really interested in an investment idea that comes your way, but not the level of risk it involves, look into other ways to enter and get some experience in its marketplace. I did a bit of research, and discovered that, if I wanted to invest in real estate, for example, I could buy a real estate investment trust index fund (REIT) which tracks stocks of companies that own apartments and shopping centers. With that investment, I would know my risks and sell my REIT shares just like a stock if I needed the money.

Figure 4.1: The lifespan of new businesses.

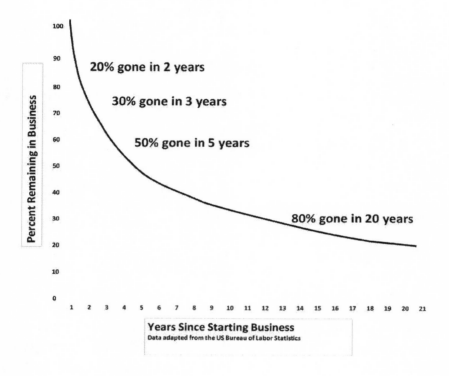

Years Since Starting Business
Data adapted from the US Bureau of Labor Statistics

As it turned out, my little Q&A session with myself paid off. I declined Morris's offer, but many of my friends and family invested in his business. My good buddy chose real estate in the wrong areas and the upgrades he made to it did little to move it, even when the real estate market continued to improve. Morris closed his venture within three years, leaving his investors with a 40% loss on their money. In that same period of time, REITs were up 86%. The math of opportunity costs clearly shows just how catastrophic this "small loss" really was for my friends and family who invested their faith—and money—in Morris.

Had one of my friends invested $10,000 in a REIT index fund in 1991 and left it there for three years, the investment would have been worth $10,000 +$10,000 X 86.06% or $18,606.00--an $8,606.00 profit. Instead, this risky business investment cost not only the $4000 that each investor didn't get back in three years, but also the profit that $10,000 could have made in an alternative, less risky, investment while your money was tied up in the house flipping project. The calculation of real loss, therefore, includes the $8,606 profit, plus the $4000 actual loss, for a total loss of $12,606.00. That's quite an opportunity cost. So, any of these investors who thought they got out of this risky business with just a $4000 loss were wrong—by over 200%.

If I really wanted to make my friends who invested in Morris's business cry, I could outline for them the long-term opportunity costs of their choice. One of my friends was only 35 years old at the time, and he believed that he could make up for the loss. He put the $6000 that he salvaged from his original investment with Morris into a REIT index fund through his IRA. Some twenty-two years later, that investment is now worth $56,305. Not bad, you might say, but consider this: Over that same 25-year period (including the three years he was invested in Morris's "flipping" business), a $10,000 original investment in an index fund would have grown in value to more than $174,600. That means my friend *really* lost $118,295 by backing Morris's failed business. That's a lot of cash down the drain.

What about 2009, when the real-estate bubble burst and the REIT index was down by as much as 37%? Doesn't matter--the average increase of REITs was almost 11% over time, and investment in those funds is spread out over multiple real-estate venues to reduce the risk of investing in a single person's ability. Morris was out of business by 1994, but the REITs marched on. So, remember: you never want to make risky investments when you are young, because you lose the ability to make a lot of money over a long period of time.

No matter what your age, you're too old to take on excessive risk. The money you lose when you're twenty-eight is money that could be earning returns for *forty years* before you retire. Every investment involves risk, but you must manage that risk at every age.

The Ultimate Challenge of Saying No to Family

Question: What is the most dangerous, potentially nasty, and absolutely-must-be-avoided-at-any-cost downside to investing with family?

Answer: Having to control your rage as you sit down to dinner with them at every post-investment family gathering.

Don't believe me. Well, let's go back to that story I outlined at the opening of this chapter, about your brother-in-law Scott, and his personal transportation device, and take a closer look at some of the potential problems that can rain down on such family linked investments.

As Scott is your brother-in-law, you and your wife know him well, both personally and socially. He's honest, reliable, and hard-working. So why is this investment such a bad risk? Let's drill deeper into this investment to find out.

We've already ticked through some of the reasons this investment is too risky: The first major problem is one of the most common among family member investors, which is that you lack intimate knowledge of the business's product and industry. What do you really know of the portable personal transportation business? You aren't likely to be knowledgeable enough about the business to make a shrewd decision about investing in it. You also know little (or nothing) about the construction, marketing, or distribution of this kind of product. Even if you studied up on those aspects of the industry, you still would know little about this product's ability to compete in a crowded field. Yes, Scott embodies some of the traits of a good entrepreneur—he's hard-working, young, good at team-building, willing to take risks, and tolerant of failure—but you don't really know how he would perform as an entrepreneur, because he has no experience in business at all. Yes, he has that MBA, but that's not the same as boots-on-the-ground experience at launching and running a business. And he's entering a highly competitive field, where that experience will matter. These are all relatively common problems that should be weighed by anyone considering investing in a family member's new business.

But the main reason you eventually should choose not to invest in Scott's business was that the risk/reward ratio it offered wasn't favorable to investors. You know that because you read Scott's prospectus and promotional material in great detail. I do this with any business investment I'm considering, and you should too, and no exceptions for family and friends. If your initial review passes muster, then you need to have a savvy business attorney examine the papers and pay that attorney well.

In the world of investing, the riskier the investment, the greater the reward it must offer to be attract investors. Here, Scott was asking $30,000 for 1% of the business, which he valued at $3,000,000, but the business had no existing plant, equipment or employees. So, what would that 1% really be worth? Investing in Scott's company involved a relatively high degree of risk but offered little in the way of reward. That made almost any less-risky investment a more attractive option, given the potential opportunity costs of tying up your money in Scott's venture versus investing in an indexed stock fund. So, high opportunity costs, limited ability to analyze the business environment, and Scott's untested entrepreneurial skills strongly suggests that this will be a high-risk venture. And those are rarely a good idea for any investor, at any age.

Finally, you really can't overlook the long-term personal fallout that will result if (when) you lose all the money you invested in Scott's business.

It may be awkward to turn down a family member's request for money, but not nearly as difficult as it will be to act like that loss didn't bother you—for the rest of your life. In this case, if you invest in Scott's business, you're very likely to lose your money, whereas, if you put that money into a reliable fund, you're much more likely to earn a profit on it. Either way, your wife is going to be unhappy. But, like many decisions in life, family investments demand that you make the best choice between two difficult alternatives. If the business takes off, great. Your family member can celebrate while your money is safely earning profits elsewhere. If the business falls into that 80% category and goes bust, however, your family member will be grateful that they don't have to feel guilty about losing your money along with theirs. Remember, you invest money to grow *your* wealth.

What happened to Scott's business?

The business stayed open for a while because its overhead was quite low, but the marketplace became increasingly competitive with a steady stream of new product releases. Scott's company sold enough units to make a small profit until 2017, when he found a buyer for the rights to manufacture the device. After that sale and the liquidation of company assets, Scott's investors received 25 cents on the dollar of their investment. In the five years that investors' money was tied up in the business, the S&P was up 81%. The stock market investment was your opportunity cost. How catastrophic was this investment? Before we leave this example, let's take a detailed look at the opportunity costs of this family investment:

Difference between S&P 500 Index price, 2011-2017   81%

Profit on $30,000 investment over that period:

(30,000 x 0.81) = $24,300;

Remains from family investment:

$30,000-22,500 = $7,500

94

What would have been your real loss on this investment? The difference between what you would have got back from your investment in Scott's business and the total you would have earned by investing in the S&P 500 Index:

$30,000 investment + $24,300 profit - $7500 actual return on family investment = $46,800

That's what you really would have lost by buying into Scott's dreams. But here's the bottom line you need to remember *any* time a family member asks you to buy into a new business: You're going to take a risk no matter what your answer. You risk alienating family members by saying no; you risk losing your money if you say yes—and that could end up causing the very rift in the family that you hoped to avoid. It doesn't matter how you're related to an entrepreneur, that person has to meet your risk standards in order to be a good candidate for your investment. You do no one a favor by losing your money along with your relatives.

Victor's Advice

Need some help coming up with the right words to kindly extricate yourself from a family member's request that you invest? Your go-to response might be, "Sorry, but I don't have the money to invest right now." If that simple statement doesn't feel like it will work, here are a few of the "no thanks" lines I've used:

"It seems like a good proposition, but I just bought (fixed up, built) a house, and that's claimed all of my available cash."

"I still have kids in college."

Or, defer to a higher authority. "MY wife/husband won't let me."

Victor's Principle #2: A Loan is an Investment

Loaning money to friends and family is another challenging situation. The more money people perceive you have the more likely it is that someone will ask you for a loan. And making those loans isn't necessarily a bad thing, in fact it can sometimes make an important difference in the health and happiness of those we love. Studies have shown that the majority of people would loan money to friends or family who were in financial trouble or ill health.[36] In fact, according to the Federal Reserve's Report on the Economic Well Being of U.S. Households in 2014, 23% of households made loans to family and friends experiencing financial hardship and more than 15% of households had received money from family and friends for a down payment on their current house. [37]

For a loan to be a *truly* kind and helpful act, though, we have to be certain that everyone involved in the arrangement is clear on its conditions. That brings us to Victor's Principle #2: A loan is an investment.

Loaning money is a tricky thing. Some loans, for example, may actually be provided as a gift to the recipient. In that case, there's rarely a discussion of the payback terms, especially if the loan is made to help a loved one through a time of extreme stress, such as the aftermath of an auto accident or death of a loved one. In the past decade, lots of Americans have loaned money to family members caught in the threat of a home foreclosure or in the wake of losing their job. Those loans can be lifesavers, but they can also present a particularly difficult situation for people on both ends of the deal. Stress levels are high, need is great, and expectations can weigh down everyone involved.

To navigate the potentially dangerous waters of a personal loan to a loved one or friend, it's important to treat that loan as an investment. As such, you need to be deliberate in the loan process. You need to be clear on what goals you have for making the loan and what conditions will help you achieve those goals, and then structure the loan accordingly. Here are six critical guidelines that can help you in that process:

1. **Be very clear about the nature of this investment.** Is it a loan, or is it a charitable gift to someone in trouble? Charity may be the right thing to do for you in a particularly difficult situation, especially if the amount of the gift is small and you do not need the money back. But, if you intend the money as a loan, you have to clearly outline the details of the arrangement including payback provisions, so that both you and the person receiving the loan understand its conditions. You should do that in the form of a written promissory note.

2. **Written promissory notes must detail the payback provisions for the loan and be signed by both borrower and lender.** Payback provisions should include when payback commences, the amount of each payment, when payments are due, and any interest or late payment penalties attached to the loan. If you're loaning a family member money to buy his or her home, you absolutely must draw up a formal note and the IRS requires that you charge some sort of interest so you will have to check their rules, though you can skip late-payment fees if you choose--you aren't a bank, after all. If the loan is intended to be used to help start a business, you also need to draw up a formal note and the provisions should include late payment penalties. You can find downloadable examples of promissory notes online, at sites such as wikidownload.com or creditcards.com.

3. **You must follow IRS rules for gifting money.** Internal Revenue Service rules limit the amount any individual can receive as a gift from another individual without paying taxes on that gift to $14,000 in a year (two parents, for example, can give a total of $28,000 without triggering a tax penalty for the gift recipient).

4. **You must pay income taxes on any interest you earn on a loan.** I loaned my daughter money to buy a house, for which I granted her the lowest published rate of interest on a 10-year loan at the time. My wife and I pay tax on the interest, but I return the interest as a gift.

5. **Be prepared for your relationship with the borrower to change.** You're now a creditor and that can stress even the strongest relationships. Your interactions at family gatherings may be less friendly, especially if there have been missed loan payments. If the loan was for a business you may feel justified in making unwelcome policy "recommendations," which also can strain the goodwill of you and your borrower. In fact, the person you loaned money to may begin to avoid you altogether. If you truly want to maintain the strength of your relationship with the borrower, you may have to work at overcoming periodic moments of awkwardness and hurt feelings.

6. **You also must be prepared for some cognitive dissonance on the part of your borrower.** Debtors don't want to think of themselves as debtors—or as loan risks. They can convince themselves that they're meeting the conditions of the loan even when they aren't. That's why your payback provisions should clearly outline the consequences of missed payments, and the types of follow-up your borrower can expect in those situations.

Let's face it—loaning money to anyone sets the stage for upheaval. Like it or not, lots of people equate money with love. If you gift money to one member of your family, others may feel slighted. Help one child buy a house, your other children see their inheritance eroding, and they blame both you and the sibling you helped. If you loan money to a married couple, you'll need to include provisions for the loan to be repaid in case they later divorce. It may seem mercenary, but your loan must be repaid before the marital assets are divided. And, don't dismiss the need for the repayment of any loan you make. You may not need the money today, but you don't know what your needs will be over the life of the loan.

Some 400 years ago, Shakespeare wrote "Neither a borrower nor a lender be." That's great advice. Loans can breed hostility and result in the loss of both the loaned money and the relationship that pre-dated the loan. We can avoid those losses, though, by understanding that a loan is an investment. As such, it demands the same amount of our time, attention, and careful structure that we would devote to any other investment. A loan or charitable gift can be a great kindness and a real source of support for someone we care about. But if we are vague or casual about the nature and conditions of the arrangement, we aren't doing *anyone* a favor.

Victor's Investment Principle #3: Invest Money to Make Money

So, we've seen that investing in risky business ventures doesn't align with the principle of investing in oneself. Even if we offer someone a personal loan, we're making an investment, so we have to be very clear about what we expect to gain (if anything) from the transaction. If we make such a deal knowing that it won't really pay us a return, then we're really talking about a gift, not an investment. That truth lies at the heart of Victor's Principle #3: You invest money to make money.

We can't spend our money before we make it, so we aren't investing in order to buy things. We invest to earn a profit. This principle is very simple and very quick to explain. In fact, we've already laid the groundwork for this principle earlier in this book.

So, to really understand the importance of this principle, let's return to what we learned in Chapter 2 about the psychology of investing. There are many reasons why people invest in losing propositions, but I've observed that many of those reasons are attached to our desire to dream of winning big. Why else would someone (like myself) buy a lottery ticket? The chances of winning are infinitesimally small, but we see those winners on TV, and we think "Wow—that could be me! Why didn't I buy that ticket?" The dream wins out over common sense, because the euphoria of the big win is so attractive. In essence, we're investing to keep a dream alive, not to make money.

That kind of wacky approach to investment isn't limited to feeding money into lottery tickets and slot machines. Remarkably, even after a big loss, many people will continue to invest in low probability return business ventures over and over again. If they've earned any money at all from one of those ventures, the memory of that win overshadows the many losses they've absorbed due to our old friend "cognitive dissonance." It may be way too painful for them to even think about where their fortunes would be if they'd socked their money in the S&P 500 index and just moved on with their life. That would have been investing money to make money—no dreams required.

Beyond the effects of cognitive dissonance, though, there's also a large dose of naiveté at work in people who willingly throw money into the black hole of risky investments. Even bad entrepreneurs can be good at selling dreams, and almost every entrepreneur believes they have a great idea. Remember, though, that you aren't investing in order to own a piece of an entrepreneur's belief, or to share in that person's shaky dream of "hitting it big." You're investing to make money. If you aren't willing to do the work necessary to completely understand the business, the market, and the finances, you can't invest. Not if you're investing to make money. Not if you want to become rich.

Victor's Investment Principle #4: The more money an investment offers, the greater the risk it involves.

Greed and the never-ending allure of a fast buck are potent weapons that can take down even savvy investors. Few of us get excited by the idea of making slow, regular investments that build money incrementally over a long period of time. Nope, we want to make a killing—a one-time, long shot investment that produces high-dollar returns *fast*. Those aggressive investment opportunities aren't hard to find, so why invest in anything else? The answer to that question lies in Victor's Principle #4: The more money an investment offers, the greater the risk it involves.

With the exception of U.S. government bonds, every investment—even an S&P 500 Index fund--involves risk. If you want to get rich you need to invest your money, so that means you have to get comfortable with some level of risk. But the higher the returns an investment offers, and the faster it offers to pay that money to investors, the more risk it involves. Only you can determine how much risk you're willing to take on, but remember this: You're investing to make money, not lose it. If you make bad investment decisions, you may end up old and broke.

Sticking to Principles

So, what's the big idea of the principles and stories we've explored in this chapter? First and foremost, we need to think carefully about the investments we make and then be brutally honest about why we're making them and what we expect to gain. A gift is a gift—if we give money to a family member or friend, we have to be willing to say good-bye to that money happily and for good. We can't set that same low bar of expectation for our investments, however.

Investments are all about making money—for *us* (*Victor's Principle #1: Invest in yourself*). They're not about "parking" our money in a savings account that earns. nothing % interest every year, and they're not about all of the stuff we want to buy with the money our money will earn (*Victor's Principle #2: Invest money to make money*). Nor should our investments be about making someone else's dreams come true. If we're making a loan, we're making an investment, so we have to be clear about its structure and provisions and get everyone to sign the documents outlining those details (*Victor's Principle #3: A loan is an investment*). And, our investment goals have to be realistic, so that our own dreams of fat, fast payoffs don't lead us to lose everything we've invested (*Victor's Principle #4: The more money an investment offers, the greater the risk it involves*).

Believe me, I know that sticking with these principles won't always be easy. But if you can truly adopt the principles I've outlined here, they can help you make even the toughest investment decisions. You'll have plenty of times when you're on the fence. But, if you apply Victor's four principles as absolute standards for any investment you make, you'll find yourself doing the groundwork necessary to help make those difficult investment calls. That means, analyzing the available information, using your judgment as you assess potential outcomes, and getting professional input and advice when necessary, then making the decision that offers the most upside for you and your money.

After you've done that groundwork, you'll be better able to live with the consequences of your decision—and, where it's necessary, you'll be able to explain your decision to friends, family members, and colleagues whose investment offers you have to refuse. If you agree to a personal or business loan, for example, you'll know that you based that decision on sound data. If you opt out, you have the same hard data to explain your decision to the would-be borrower. In other words, these principles can help minimize any regrets over the investment decisions you've made.

Along with my four principles of investment, the stories we've explored in this chapter illustrate some important points for any new investor:

1. The majority of new businesses fail in the short run, and up to 80% of new businesses are gone in 20 years. We're almost always better off investing in indexed stock funds than in new business ventures.
2. Investing in family may appease our spouse, mother, brother, or other relative, but those are risky investments that can end up losing both our money and our family's good will. Ditto investing with friends; we run the risk of being a double loser.
3. Losing money when we're young is very costly.
4. Following a firm set of investment principles can help us have the guts to say NO when those around us are encouraging us to say YES.
5. We make more money by saying NO than yes.

Yes, it's much easier to turn down a request for investment in a risky business startup from someone we don't know or care about than it is to say NO to someone we love or admire. But it's no more important. Lost money is lost money, and that's not what investing is all about. So, remember my investment principles, do your homework, take a deep breath, and say NO if the numbers and other data don't add up. The statistics are in your favor.

Chapter 5: Saying NO to the "house investment" myth

Back in 2002, I lived in an old house that sat on a beautiful 2-acre lakeside lot in one of the most prosperous suburbs of Detroit. After much consideration, my wife and I scrapped the house we hated and, in its place, built a house that was better suited to its neighborhood and that better matched our taste and needs. My stock broker Alex, who like me was in his 50s, with three children at home, loved our new house and its location. While discussing financial markets one night he announced that he and his wife were going to buy a lot and build in Grosse Point, an upscale city near Detroit. Alex had an income of $500,000 a year, would have no trouble getting a building loan. He couldn't find a great lot he could afford on Lake St. Clair so he purchased a smaller parcel away from the water. Alex and his wife felt that they could live with the lot, especially if they could build the house of their dreams upon it. Alex had talked with the bank, and was a bit taken aback when presented with the news that his monthly mortgage would be around $14 ,000. "It's a big investment, but I can afford it," he told me at lunch one day, "and the house is exactly what we want. I haven't signed the papers on any of this yet—what do you think?" I knew Alex was primed to make this deal and really just wanted some unconditional support for the move. But was it a good deal?

Answer: NO!

I'm all for spending your money on the place you live. At the same time, Alex wasn't making an investment—he was taking on a massive expense for a commodity that may or may not be worth as much to anyone else as it was to Alex. Not everyone would want a large house on a lot located some distance from the area's most appealing feature; water). In spite of his high-paying job, Alex hadn't amassed significant wealth. If he lost his job, he would have to sell the place, and who would be willing to pay what he had already "invested" in it? I didn't want to throw cold water on Alex's happy plans, but I told him to be careful, because "you never know what might happen." I also told him that I didn't think of houses as investments, but as expenses, something you need and buy and then when you don't need them you sell them and hope to get your money back. I didn't think "hope" was a strong enough lifeline for such a large and risky expenditure.

In the end, Alex built the house—and then needed that lifeline. He lost his job, just as the housing crisis cranked into full gear. In his field and at his income level, replacement jobs were hard to come by. And in a rapidly decaying market, there were no takers for his expensive house away from the area's biggest draw, views of Lake St. Claire. In short, Alex was underwater on his mortgage, and had to move his family to a more affordable home. Although he eventually landed a job in another investment firm, the financial hit he took during his foreclosure has left a permanent hole in his net worth--the opportunity cost of the hundreds of thousands of dollars he "invested" in his dream home. Alex was totally right choosing the neighborhood in which to build his dream house as schools and property values in Grosse Point were prime. The fact that the economy imploded at time he built his dream home was bad luck...but was a risk that is taken by too many who build a dream house and spend more than they can ultimately afford.

The first thing you need to know about buying a house is that it's the largest and most important purchase you will ever make. If you're going to spend some money, this is where you do it. And, I'm not talking about spending on the size of the home, the magnificence of its professional kitchen, or the grandness of its master suite. While you need to buy a home with a layout and design that works for you, nothing that's in your home matters as much as what's outside it. By that, I mean the neighborhood. When you buy a house, you're really buying the neighborhood it sits in. Where you live defines in many ways your financial and social status, your social life, and the places where you'll worship, shop, and recreate. Your home's location also determines how far you have to commute to work each day. A significant number of patients in my sleep disorders practice complain of fatigue, and commuting is often the culprit. It's not uncommon for working people to commute 45 minutes to an hour each way. Flex hours, telecommuting, even public transportation can lessen this problem, but those arrangements can change in a heartbeat; your neighborhood location can't. Even more critically, your location also will play a major role in determining where your kids will go to school, the quality of the education they'll receive, the after-school activities they'll participate in, and the people they'll hang out with. Any of those variables is important; together, they represent some of the most critical factors in life.

Your neighborhood also will determine how satisfied you are with your daily life. Will you be able to walk the streets safely at night and park your car on the street? Will your neighbors love to store RVs in their driveways and host loud parties all summer? Are the lots so small that the air conditioning system next door is right outside your window, where it can share its motor noise with you all summer long? Do you get to wake up to the drone of low-flying planes landing at a nearby airport at 3 a.m.? These aren't trivial issues. You could live in a palace, but if the neighborhood is crowded, noisy, poorly maintained, or home to other ongoing factors that annoy you, you're going to be unhappy. That's why I advise my students and interns who are ready to buy their first home to be prepared to spend what it takes to get into a neighborhood that meets *all* of their essential criteria.

All that being said, however, the next most important thing you need to know about buying a house is that it's a commodity, not an investment. Remember Victor's Principle #3: *You invest money to make money.* When we account for inflation, most homes simply maintain their value over time. In fact, take a look at Figure 5.1, which is a summary of Case-Shiller housing price data for the past 120 years or so.[38] This housing price index, hosted and maintained by Standard & Poor's, tracks U.S. housing prices nationally and in twenty urban areas. As the data shows, taking inflation into account, the value of homes hasn't changed much over that time, with the exception of the spike in housing prices that created the housing bubble and the vertiginous drop in prices between 2009 and 2012, after the bubble burst. With the low interest rates and improved economy that followed those years, however, housing prices rebounded significantly.

Given this century-long period of relative stability in home prices, it's reasonable to expect that prices are going to level out again at historic returns. You might make real money on your house if you live in New York City, San Francisco, Boston, or other areas where prices have significantly outpaced the average *and* if you haven't lavishly overspent on the purchase and improvement of your property. The rest of us, though, shouldn't count on a windfall when we sell, or expect to retire on the value of our house. If we live there long enough and do a reasonably good job of maintenance and updates, our house likely will increase in value along with inflation, just like many other commodities. If we do end up raking in a pile of money by selling our home, well, it's a bonus.

Figure 5.1: Housing Price Data from 1890 to 2016.

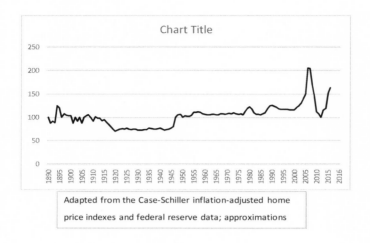

One thing Figure 5.1 doesn't show is how much the average home has changed since 1890. Indoor plumbing, electricity, air conditioning, in-ground pools—our homes today include a lot more amenities and, as a result, require that much more expense for basic care and maintenance. The demographics of the average homebuyer have changed dramatically, as well. People change jobs more often, so they move more often. Buyers are a diverse lot, too, with a growing number of single people, unmarried couples, and DINCs (double income, no children) looking for homes *and* neighborhoods that fit their lifestyle. All of these changes have contributed to a shift in the American Dream, particularly as it applies to home ownership.

All of those changes mean that nearly *everyone* in America will face some fundamental questions of home ownership at some point in their life: Is it time to buy a home? Should I forget about owning and rent? Should I buy *this* home? How much is it really going to cost? How about a vacation home—will it be worth the cost (and hassle)? In this chapter, we're going to look at some of the hard data that can help find answers to those difficult, and often emotional, questions. You may not need all of the information and ideas in this chapter right now, but you very likely will at some point in the not too distant future. Owning a home can be an almost primordial urge, so it pays to have the information necessary to make a detached, unemotional "YES" or "NO" decision about the purchase. That same knowledge also can help you if you're getting ready to sell a home.

So, if your home isn't an investment, why are we talking about it? The answer is simple: I've included this chapter to give you information that can help you make smart spending decisions when it comes to one of the largest expenditures you'll ever be tempted to make. Armed with the data and ideas we'll cover here, you'll be better able to say NO to housing costs that you really can't, shouldn't, or don't want to take on, and use the money you save to say YES to the *real* investment opportunities that come your way.

Victor's Advice

Buying a home is the largest expenditure most of us will ever make, so the decision can't be based on nostalgia, tradition, gut feeling, or common wisdom. Do your homework, run the numbers, and let facts, not emotion, guide your choices.

Renting Versus Buying

To rent or buy? Beyond a desire to put down roots, there are a number of important considerations you need to wrestle with when you're answering that question. Buying certainly does offer some advantages. Under the current IRS rules, for example, interest payments on the first $1.1 million of a loan are tax deductible. That can make home ownership a better financial deal than renting, especially if you're in a higher tax bracket and intend to live in one place for the long haul. Even with the down payment and average maintenance expenses, if you're able to stay in the residence for four or more years, you stand a good chance of breaking even or turning a small profit when you sell, depending on your timing and the housing market. And, it's easier to buy than rent in the best neighborhoods. People who live in great neighborhoods don't move as often, and when they do, they typically want to sell their house, not hang onto it and take on the hassles of being a landlord.

Home ownership also comes with its own set of disadvantages. First, it can be really expensive. There's the opportunity cost of tying up cash in down payment expenses, which could be 5% or more of the price you pay for the home. That's money you could have invested (and earned a profit on) elsewhere. And then there are the related expenses, such as property taxes, home-owners association fees, private mortgage insurance, and above all, maintenance. A common rule of thumb says you should count on spending 1% of your home's value on maintenance every year, but a lot of homeowners will tell you that their maintenance expenses climb even higher. If you do the work yourself, you'll have materials expenses and a lot of hours devoted to maintenance chores. Hire it done, and maintenance becomes even more expensive. The larger the house and the more amenities it offers, the more maintenance it will require.

If you're early in your career and expect to go where the best job offers may take you over the next ten years, you'll have to sell your home in order to move on. Selling a house can be difficult—and expensive. You'll pay a realtor's commission of 5-6% of your home's selling price, and your closing costs could tack on another 2% or so to those costs. You have no idea what shape the housing market will be in when you're ready to sell, so you may lose some money in a down-market, as well. As we've seen, history tells us that our house is likely to maintain its value over time, but unexpected spikes and drops in home values do occur.

That brings us to the advantages of renting. When the lease is up, you can leave the area with only your moving expenses to account for. Or, worst case scenario, you pay a fee to break the lease. Even if that fee is high, it still offers you the freedom to pick up and go where opportunity beckons. Renting also gives you a chance to try out a type of home or even a neighborhood where you may—or may not—want to sink your money and roots. Renting is particularly advantageous when you're young and both your needs and finances are still in flux. If your income rises quickly, you can upgrade to a better home quickly, too, without worrying whether your current home's value has appreciated or depreciated. You aren't on the hook for maintenance issues, so you don't have to worry about unexpected home problems making a major dent in your wallet when you least expect or can afford it. And the money you would have spent on a mortgage down payment can be efficiently earning money in an investment account instead.

Most of us are renters at some point in our life, and so we know the disadvantages of that arrangement, most of which revolve around the instability of living in someone else's property. Rent can go up every year, and those raises may not be regulated so you have no idea what your living expenses will be in the years to come. You're dependent on the landlord to make necessary improvements, and you can't really control the quality or timing of the work. Some landlords require that you do your own lawn maintenance and snow removal, and you may be on the hook for all utilities other than water and garbage pickup. And landlords can find ways to break leases just as tenants do. If housing prices skyrocket in your neighborhood, the landlord may decide it's time to sell and get out of the renting business. When that happens, you'll have a period of time to get out, but you *will* have to move (unless you want to cough up the money to buy the property with its newly hefty price tag). The better the neighborhood, the fewer and more expensive the rentals will be.

While some aspects of renting versus buying are based strictly on housing and lifestyle preferences, we can compare the costs to add some clear-cut evidence to our decisions. You can use any of the numerous online calculators to plug in numbers and estimate home purchase costs based on current interest rates, your tax bracket, what you could get on your investments, expected maintenance costs, and, very importantly, at what level the house might appreciate.[39] Some even allow you to calculate a rent-versus-buy comparison.

The real question to ask yourself as you make these calculations is whether buying is worth the effort and expense, based on how long you expect to remain in the home. That timeline really shapes the level of risk you're taking with this expenditure. And remember, if you lose or are forced to change your job, you may have to sell sooner than you had planned, perhaps at a loss. In many cases, unless you feel very certain that you aren't going to have (or want) to move for at least six or more years, renting may be the simplest *and* most cost-effective option.

Getting rid of the idea of our house as an investment is important because it enables us to see our home for what it really is—the place where we live. Depending on how long we live there, we may or may not get back the money we spend on buying, insuring, and maintaining a home. But we most definitely will live with the realities of our home's location, and those realities very likely will play a role in how easily we can sell our house when we're ready to move, and how much we can sell it for. When you're making your own decisions about renting versus buying a home, take all of these factors into account. Figure out the true costs in both time and money and assess how well those costs fit with your overall budget and lifestyle. Then, make your decisions to buy or rent based on those facts, rather than reverting to the 20th century common wisdom that everyone should own their own home and buying is more cost-efficient than renting. It's your money, and you should spend it in a way that best fits your tax bracket, your financial situation, and your career and family plans.

Victor's Advice

Be aware that your down payment is sunk in the house and you cannot invest the sum elsewhere for profits. The down payment is an opportunity cost of buying a home and must be factored into the cost of ownership.

Yes or No: A Checklist for Home Buyers

Let's say you've decided it's time to buy—now what? Most real estate professionals agree that location is the prime consideration when buying a house. We've already discussed some of the most critical neighborhood factors that you need to consider when deciding whether or not to buy a specific home. Those include:

- ✓ **The school system**: Even if you don't have kids who will attend local schools, the quality of those schools can affect both the price and sale-ability of your home.
- ✓ **The neighborhood and the immediate neighbors:** A great house in a neighborhood that's incompatible with your lifestyle preferences is no bargain, no matter how little it costs.
- ✓ **The commute:** If you spend too much of your time getting to and from work, you won't really have much opportunity to appreciate the greatness of your neighborhood *or* your home.

These aren't the only critical issues you'll need to consider, though. When I was a poor student, I vowed I would have three things in a house: A garage, because I never wanted to be scraping ice off a car before going to work; someone to care for the lawn and plants so I had more time to do the things I liked; and a place to put the trash so I did not have to wrestle garbage cans down to the street every week. That's me. You'll have your own requirements for any new house you're considering, but here's a quick list of things I think anyone will want to keep in mind when shopping for a new home:

✓ **Is it the most expensive house in the neighborhood?** Those houses can be hard to resell, and your neighbors have less financial incentive than you do to keep the neighborhood clean and well-maintained.

✓ **Is it on a busy road, close to a noisy bar or restaurant, or in the path of an airport?** Even people who claim noise doesn't bother them can find themselves tired and foggy during the day because they simply can't rest well at night. Drive the neighborhood at night and on weekends to get a sense of what it's like when people are at home and active. Definitely meet the neighbors.

✓ **Is the neighborhood full of rental properties?** Rentals can change occupants frequently, and that means you could have a parade of new neighbors each year.

✓ **Do the house layout and amenities match your lifestyle?** Do you need a big kitchen for entertaining or to feed a large family? Do you want an open floor plan versus a collection of rooms that can be closed off from each other? Can you afford the changes you would feel compelled to make? Will you need zoning permits? Are there historic neighborhood restrictions?

✓ **Does it have the amount of space you need—including storage space?** I live in Michigan where basements are desirable and not infrequently become areas of storage. No basement? Look to attic space or the garage. Garage space is important not just for cars. Where do you put trash? The extra refrigerator and freezer?

✓ **Will landscaping be a major issue?** Tree removal can be very expensive, so if the house is on a lot with many trees, you may want to have them inspected. Who is going to mow the lawn and care for the plants?

✓ **What does it cost to run the place?** Ask for tax and utility bills, and don't forget cable and internet access. Tax bills usually run about one percent of the value of the house per year, but you'll want to find out what the rate is and if any recent increases have been approved. Heating bills are one indicator of how well the house is insulated.

✓ **Is there deferred maintenance you'll need to catch up?** How soon will the house need a new roof, new furnace, new electrical service or wiring, plumbing, water or sewer line repairs? Does it need new windows? Any of these repairs or upkeep issues can be extremely expensive—and a real deal-breaker. Use a reputable home inspector, go through the house with them, and ask questions.

✓ **How close are you to essential services, such as medical care, police, and fire stations**? Too close to a fire station or emergency room, and you'll be jolted awake by sirens every time those services get called into use. Too far from a fire station—or hydrant—and you may get hit with extra home insurance charges.

✓ **Has the house had recent insurance claims?** See if you can get a CLUE (Comprehensive Loss Underwriting Exchange) report from the owner which comes from a database insurance companies use to rate policies. Most states require home owners to complete a disclosure statement revealing major problems such as termites, water damage, or hazardous conditions such as wildfires and flooding.

Finally, is everyone who will be living in the home on board with its purchase? If you buy a home that your spouse, partner, or even your older children don't want to live in, you'll pay for it every time there's a problem with the house or the neighborhood. Maybe you won't care about that but living with people who are unhappy with their home can be stressful for everyone involved.

Protect Yourself with Experienced Help

Some people like to think of themselves as fabulous deal-makers, but the best deal-makers always get the best professional advice. If you're a first-time home buyer, you should never go it alone. You're going to spend a lot of money on this purchase, and there are many ways it can go wrong. You'll be signing lots of paperwork, negotiating a lot of expenses, and committing to a deal that will stay with you for as long as you are paying on your home (and the opportunity costs of buying it). The most effective way to make smart choices during this process is to get expert help to guide you through it.

If you're new to home buying, consider having an experienced family member or friend look at any house you think you want to buy. Years ago, my wife and I were ready to buy our first home, a charming house in the hills overlooking romantic Napa, California, where I was practicing. One of our older, more experienced friends said "Don't buy it. It's too far from town and not near any schools or shopping." We hated to pass up the place, but decided my friend was right. We bought in a sub-division instead, and when I had to sell the house two years later, we sold at a profit—because of the great schools nearby. Meanwhile, the charming house was up for sale again and had been on the market for more than four months at the time we sold our house.

When my daughter got ready to buy her first house, I was able to pass along my own experienced advice. She was already interested in a house that had a "water view," which actually meant it was one of many houses bordering a free-standing pond. I walked through it with her and saw multiple signs that the house had been renovated by a do-it-yourselfer—unfinished flooring transitions, poor trim work, and so on—that she really hadn't noticed. I told her to avoid buying someone else's poor handiwork, which undoubtedly extended beyond those surface problems. She liked the house but agreed that she didn't want to fix a parade of problems down the road, and so she passed on it. I later was able to help her land a house she *really* wanted. Bidding was fast and furious for homes in the area, so I was able to help my daughter make a decision and move quickly on a good deal in a competitive market. Don't be afraid to ask experienced family and friends for their help. They've needed it in the past and typically are happy to share their advice and experiences.

Even with a savvy friend or relative, though, you should find a good realtor to help you through the search and purchase of a new home. Like any other service, a realtor's references and reputation are important. Do some online research, check out what previous clients have said, and then interview at least two or three realtor candidates. Choose one with a sound reputation, but also make sure you're comfortable with that person and their approach to the job. If you don't like the realtor or don't feel that you're getting the attention you need, move on. Remember, though, the realtor makes his or her living by selling homes, not showing them.

Then there's the loan. Some of my biggest hassles, both emotional and legal, have been with loan companies. Again, do your homework to find a reputable company--and check references. Your realtor has a vested interest in closing the deal quickly, and he or she is likely to know the lenders in the area who are reliable and fast. Even then, you need to check the recommended lender's references online, and search for filed complaints with the National Association of Realtors, local and state realtor associations, and with the Better Business Bureau. You can't make your choice based on the lender's costs and interests rates alone. I thought I was so smart about 15 years ago, when I sent out letters to a number of loan companies asking about their lowest interest rate on a 30-year conventional mortgage. I didn't bother checking references. I chose the company with the lowest interest rate and locked it in. When interest rates went up, the loan company started dragging its feet on finalizing the loan. Finally, I fired them and got a loan from another company. I won a lawsuit on this one because my credit was impeccable, but the process was long, tedious, and wearing. This lender was out of business in a few years, and I learned my lesson about judging a lender on rates, alone.

You also need to take the time to read the mortgage papers and make sure they specify the agreed-upon rate. Years ago, I paid an attorney to review mortgage papers for me and verify that they were in order. Nevertheless, on the day of the closing, I insisted on reading through all of the paperwork I was being asked to sign and discovered that the lender had raised the interest rate an 1/8 of a point—a change my attorney had failed to notice. A small percentage point can mean a lot of money on a 30-year mortgage. That experience taught me a lesson; do your homework, find a reputable lender, and then read the documents thrust at you across the table during the closing.

Victor's Advice

When you are in the process of getting approval for a loan, don't make any big purchases. They can affect your credit and may slow the loan process.

Mortgage interest rates vary, based on the length and conditions of the loan, with short-term ARMs (adjustable rate mortgages) sometimes offering dramatically lower rates than a traditional 15 or 30-year mortgage. Before you sign on for an ARM loan, though, you need to be very certain that your finances will flex along with the loan rate if you stay in the home longer than the initial rate period. In the recent housing crisis, many people got short 5- or 7-year ARM loans, then couldn't afford the rate hike when it hit. Many of those folks had to default on their loans, and thus lost their home and everything they'd sunk into it during the time they lived there. That outcome was a losing situation for everyone, including the individuals involved, the neighborhoods that became pocked with foreclosures, and the economy, which weakened under the skyrocketing numbers of loan defaults.

Parsing the many types of mortgages you can choose from and the subtleties of interest rates are topics too complex to discuss here. I can offer you this bottom line, though: Don't allow yourself to be charmed or rushed into a decision as important as a home purchase. Research your realtor and lender, understand your interest rate and the provisions of your loan, know what you can afford and when you can afford it. Most importantly, get good expert help throughout the process, and don't be afraid to ask questions. That's the smart way to spend your money.

No, You Don't Need a Second Home

Like a buying a boat or joining a country club, buying a vacation home can be a very compelling idea for anyone whose income has advanced into the "beyond comfortable" range. If you're a multi-millionaire who spends a great deal of time at a vacation spot, entertaining large groups of people for extended stays there, then maybe a vacation home would be a good idea. But, I've spent a good deal of time calculating the costs and benefits of a second home, and the numbers are clear; for most people, most of the time, buying a second or vacation home or condo is a bad deal.

For example, let's suppose you buy a condominium in Florida for $200,000. In addition to your down payment (which I assume will be 20%), you'll get tagged for 2% of the home's purchase price at closing, for costs such as an 'origination fee", processing fees, appraisals, credit report, attorney's fees, flood certification, and property mortgage insurance. Those costs vary, but you can assume they'll push your home's cost to about $204,000. In addition to your mortgage, you'll have operation costs such as property taxes, homeowner's association (HOA) fees, utilities, homeowner's insurance, and any maintenance expenses not covered by your HOA agreement. Here's what you might expect in your first year's expenses:

Down payment + 2%: $44,000

Annual mortgage payments: $9021

Operation cost: $22,171

Total cost year 1: $67,171

While they won't include the down payment and closing costs, your second-year annual maintenance costs will be even higher. Factoring in a 3% inflation rate and the opportunity cost of tying up your money in something other than an interest-earning investment, those second-year costs come to $24,778. That figure will continue to increase yearly by 3%.

The average American takes 16.2 vacation day a year, but let's say that you plan to spend at a month at your vacation home that first year. In that case, your daily rate for using the condo would be just over $1180. A quick look on the Vacation Rentals by Owner website (www.vrbo.com) shows that you can rent a high-quality, three bedroom, two-bath vacation property in a Florida resort town for $4500 a month or less than $150 a day. You would need to use your purchased vacation condo *every day* during that first year to reduce its daily cost to that of our $150-a-day sample rental. During the second year, you'd need to stay at your vacation home for almost six months to even get close to the sample rental costs. So, unless you plan to be on vacation for the majority of the year, *and* you are certain that you'll never want to vacation anywhere else, owning that vacation condo makes no economic sense.

The opportunity costs of ownership make having that vacation condo even less inviting. I'm going to make some broad assumptions here, including that real estate increases in value at the historic norm of the rate of inflation, and that an investment in the S&P 500 earns its historic return of 10% and that you deduct your interest payments from taxes and then sell the condo at the end of 10 years. With those assumptions, an investment in an S&P 500 index fund of the money spent on the second home's mortgage payments and upkeep costs as we've outlined them would have brought in $330,490 which would translate into $1065 per use day if you are using the place 4 weeks a year. That's a stiff opportunity cost, and a handsome price to pay for a little-used getaway spot. Of course, if the stock market tanked and prices of Florida property went much higher, you may well come out ahead. But, it's no wonder that so many people are so happily renting out their second houses and condos online. (Be aware, of course, that if you rent out your condo, you now are operating it as a business, and so will need to account for that income at tax time.)

As for me, I don't like to take big risks for uncertain rewards, so I'll rent a vacation spot. I recommend you consider that option too when you find yourself leaning toward buying a second home. As you get closer to retirement, you can rent a vacation home for a month or two—or even a season--in different places to see where you might like to spend your leisure time. Then, when you're able to spend a more substantial period of time there, you can consider owning your own place in paradise.

I'm not trying to rain on family vacations, but this chapter is about making solid a financial decision on our largest purchases. Eventually, all of our dreams collide with reality, and this is one dream that could result in financial nightmare. Rent until you are certain about your needs and forget about what you *want* to believe about the luxurious life of second-home-ownership.

Making Your Home Work for Your Long-Term Wealth Plan

Speaking of dreams, this entire chapter has been devoted to helping you wake up to the realities that surround the great American Dream of owning a home. Our home is much more than the space in which we live; it also can shape our social life, our family life, our work life, our finances, and our very concept of who we are and what kind of world we occupy. But understanding what a home *isn't* is just as important. A home isn't necessarily where we will live forever. Nor is it a hermetically sealed bubble that can shield us from the realities of the neighborhood in which it stands. Above all, it isn't a reliable vehicle for building wealth. Yes, our home may increase in value and, in that way, contribute toward our overall net worth. But we need to buy or rent a home based on our needs, our existing finances, and our short and long-term plans for where and how we want to live. Remember, a home is not an investment.

As we've seen in this chapter, buying a home requires us to answer a long list of questions about our needs, plans, and priorities. To help organize your thoughts on these questions, here are a few short lists that summarize the advice we've explored here about how to make a YES or NO call when looking for a home.

Say YES to:

- The best neighborhood
- The best school system
- Comparing costs and convenience of renting versus buying
- A good realtor
- Needs, not lofty desires
- A workable floor plan
- Adequate storage
- Essential spaces (master bedroom, baths, kitchen) that match your needs
- A reputable lender

Say NO to:

- Outsized dreams and emotional decisions
- The biggest and best house in the neighborhood
- Obnoxious neighbors
- Busy/noisy streets and neighborhood
- Too many rentals nearby
- Necessary improvements that go beyond your financial limitations and levels of tolerance
- Influence of the previous owner's décor
- Large purchases during loan approval and closing process
- A second home that you'll use infrequently

Despite common wisdom, owning a home isn't always the best option for stabilizing our life *or* saving money. Our home is where we live, and our decision to buy a home—or not—needs to be geared toward supporting the best life we can have now and building the best future we can envision down the road.

CHAPTER 6: SAY NO TO INVESTMENT SCAMS

You're invited to a party hosted by a member of your country club. When you arrive, you realize that you don't 'really know many of the people there, so you're especially happy when another of the guests walks over and starts a casual conversation with you about the club, the host's neighborhood, and work—the usual social chatter. When you mention that you're a doctor, your new acquaintance remarks that he works with several members of your occupation, some of whom are at the party that night, because he's an investment advisor who specializes in wealth management for members of the medical profession. He quickly changes the subject to other topics then, before drifting back toward the drinks table, he hands you his card and tells you to get in touch some time so you two can play a round of golf at the club. You do, and within a few months you two have become regular golf buddies. On the course one day, you ask him about the type of investments he's handling and whether there are any you should buy into. He waves the question away, but when you press him for ideas, he tells you he'll keep his eyes open. A few weeks later, you get a late-night Friday call from him: "Look, you said you were interested, so I wanted to let you know about a deal that some of the other guys at our club have jumped on. It's going to be fast and dirty. I've got wind of a biotech firm that's about to go public; I think we could pull in maybe a 28% return by buying now. I can get you in, but you have to act quickly. If you want in, get me a check by Monday, and I'll take care of it. If not, no problem— just forget about this call. The fewer people discussing this deal, the better." You're on a long shift over the weekend and won't have time to dig into the details of this deal, but you're very interested.

Question: Should you consider just going ahead and investing some small amount, so you don't lose out entirely on this 28% return?

Answer: NO! As we've learned in previous chapters, opportunity costs give even small investments large repercussions. Even more importantly, what this guy's suggesting smacks of insider trading. Let's say the deal works out and you do score a fat return—which is highly unlikely. You're now in business with someone untrustworthy, and that's not the kind of person you want to hand over your money to. If you want to invest safely, sensibly, and profitably, you need to form and follow an investment plan, rather than plunking down money on any scheme that comes your way. And if you're going to look for investment advice, do your homework first, to make sure the one advising you is licensed, registered, experienced, and hasn't been the source of client complaints.

Volatile markets, shifting economies, risky business ventures—a lot of factors threaten investors today. But, in a crowded universe of financial black holes, investment scams are among the most difficult investment problems to avoid. The world seems to be crawling with scam artists, and investment schemes can be a scammer's dream come true. Lots of money can change hands very quickly, while the scam itself can remain under the radar for a long period of time. When the inevitable moment of reckoning arrives, and victims are faced with the irrefutable evidence that their trusted adviser/friend/investment partner is a fraud, many are reluctant to admit that they've fallen for a hoax. Even worse, if the heat starts to rise, the crooks can simply change their names, addresses, and cover stories, and reel in a whole new group of victims.

Make no mistake, it's very easy to become one of those victims. Scams emerge, flourish, and change forms on what seems like a daily basis, defying our ability to identify, track, and uproot them. The thieves promoting these frauds can flawlessly project honesty, sincerity, and a deep interest in your financial success, even as they steal you blind. If you think you'd be able to spot these scam artists and their schemes, think again. Bernie Madoff didn't get rich stealing from gullible, greedy idiots; his victims included international banking institutions, investment firms, insurance companies, pension funds, university endowments, and well-known professional athletes, actors, and business owners. Madoff's web captured seasoned financial professionals and rookie investors alike, and every victim baited the trap for the next.

That's how the best scams work, and they succeed at every level of society. Success breeds success. The more marks an investment scammer pulls in, the easier it is to attract an even bigger crowd. You don't need to hang out at the country club or with the well-heeled crowd on Fifth Avenue or Wall Street to get roped in by an investment scammer, either. Social media has become a favored hunting ground for the world's fast-growing population of scam artists and scoundrels. If you're on Facebook, LinkedIn, Twitter, or any popular social media platform, some scammer somewhere just may have your number.

It's a jungle out there for investors, folks, and in this chapter, we're going to explore the hunting habits of some of its most dangerous predators--and how to avoid becoming their prey. The shady individuals and organizations who cultivate the world's flourishing undergrowth of investment scams and schemes are masters of reinvention and deception. Here, we'll examine how to see through their disguises and how to spot a scam being promoted by good, decent people who have unknowingly fallen into the clutches of a financial fraudster and are, in turn, encouraging others to join them. Finally, we'll walk through some smart steps for avoiding shady financial advisors and for identifying just how closely we fit the profile of Investment Scammer Victim #1. Like it or not, we *all* can wear that label at one time or another. After all, if it were easy to say NO to scams, there wouldn't be so many of them out there.

Reviewing the Rogue's Lineup of Investment Fraud

Lots of people have invested money in stocks, funds, bonds, and other vehicles that have ultimately failed to pay off. There's no shame in that; as we've said before, if there are no risks involved, it's not an investment. Losing money on a miscalculation is one thing; having that money stolen from you through fraudulent promises and practices is another beast altogether. In previous chapters, we've explored lots of ways to vet and select investments, so that we can avoid losing everything in a bad call. Now, let's take a look at how to spot a stone-cold scam so we can avoid becoming its victim.

While, like bacteria, scams grow, spread, and change forms with such rapidity that we'll never be able to list and describe them all, most investment scams are variations on a few common types:

- **Ponzi Schemes** in which smooth-talking scam artists pay "dividends" to old investors with new investors' money, while never actually investing *anyone's* money and keeping most of *everyone's* money for themselves; when the scheme runs out of new investors, the money flow stops and everyone (but the scam artist) loses. A variation on this scam is the **pyramid scheme**, in which people are recruited as salespeople for a product or service, when in fact, the real goal of the operation is to collect the recruit's investment in fees for initial set-up and stocking, and then to encourage that person to recruit more people to similarly "invest." The promoter offers to share with the recruit the "investment" of all the new recruits he or she brings in—thus putting the "pyramid" in pyramid schemes.

- **Affinity Schemes** in which scammers target a specific group of people to invest in a bogus fund or stock. Typically, the scam artist gets a respected member of the group or community to invest, makes sure that individual sees strong "returns" (at least for a while), then relies on that person's open discussion and praise of the investment to sell it to others in the group. Meanwhile, the scammer pockets all of the money brought in by new investors.
- **Pump and dump schemes** in which scam artists, typically one or more investors, buy up numerous shares of a relatively worthless stock, hype the stock wildly to new investors, then sell off all of their shares when they've succeeded in driving the stock's price through the roof. After the sell-off, the stock's price tanks. The scammers score a handsome profit, while new investors are left holding stock that may be worth just pennies on the dollar of their original investment.

Now, let's take a closer look at the lineup of these classic investment scams before we overview some of the most effective ways to avoid them.

The Ponzi Scheme: Get rich quick!

The Ponzi scheme is named after a 19th century fraudster, Charles Ponzi. An immigrant from Italy, Ponzi was involved in number of minor schemes and scams around the United States before he stumbled onto the "big one" that brought him fortune—and infamy. The scheme that ended up making Ponzi's name a household word began in 1918 and revolved around a scam in which he purported to buy postal reply coupons in a foreign country, and then make a healthy profit by redeeming them in the United States for more money than their purchase price. Ponzi claimed to have a group of agents working for his enterprise in various locations around Europe and promised investors in his "business" a 50% profit in 40-45 days. [40] In spite of the fact that he lured in nearly 40,000 investors, there was no enterprise, just a lot of shuffled money and fraudulent claims. Ponzi paid off the first round of investors and occasionally made large (and well-publicized) payments to others along the way. For the most part, though, he merely pocketed the money his marks "invested" in his business. By the time his scheme blew up in 1920, Ponzi was believed to have cost his investors as much as $20,000,000.[41] Ponzi went to jail, and later died a pauper. While Ponzi didn't invent this particular type of scam, his success at it permanently linked the scheme to his name.

Some 100 years later, the Ponzi scheme remains a favorite of scam artists around the world. Old investors are paid with new investors' money, and the scam artists get rich by pocketing their own big chunk of the money that's passing through. While the U.S. Security and Exchange Commission (SEC) continues to root out and eliminate Ponzi scheme investment scams, they continue to pop up. The *Financial Times* reported one such scam in 2017, which involved luring investors to buy into a supposed secondary market for tickets to big-name entertainment venues, such as the Broadway musical *Hamilton* and concerts by artists such as Bob Dylan and the Rolling Stones. If you think that sounds like a weird business to be in, you're right. Nevertheless, the SEC credited the scheme with scamming almost $81,000,000 from approximately 125 investors.[42] This kind of odd "business" as a basis for an investment vehicle should be a red flag for potential investors.

One of the most famous crooks to run a Ponzi scheme was Bernard Madoff, the New York investment advisor whose multibillion dollar investment firm was nothing more than a giant Ponzi scheme. Madoff's list of victims is impressive, including names such as the Royal Bank of Scotland Group PLC, the French Bank Credit Agricole SA, director/producer/philanthropist Steven Spielberg, and the Elie Wiesel Foundation.[43] When Madoff was unable to raise enough new money to keep his investors from growing suspicious, the scheme imploded—but not before Madoff had bilked investors of almost $65 billion. He pleaded guilty to 11 felony counts in 2009 and was sentenced to 150 years in prison. At the time of this writing, Madoff is 79 years old and still serving out his sentence.

Like Charles Ponzi and Bernard Madoff, the con men and women who run Ponzi schemes tend to be charismatic and convincing. Many boldly run ads in legitimate media for their fake businesses to give them an air of legitimacy. These scam investments almost always offer the promise of high returns in a short period of time and at extremely low risk and, like Madoff's crooked enterprise, they go after smart people with a lot of money. If you fit that description, be on the lookout for charming, seemingly respectable investment "experts" offering to let you in on a deal that seems too good to be true.

Victor's Advice

Information is everything, and the web holds a lot of information about Ponzi schemes and their makers. If you're interested in reading up on the ever-expanding list of Ponzi scheme scam artists being brought under prosecution, you can visit www.ponzitracker.com, a site run by Tampa attorney and white-collar crime expert, John Maglich, who also contributes articles to *Forbes* magazine, with a focus on Ponzi schemes.

Affinity Fraud: We're All in This Together

One of the most common investment scams is known as *affinity fraud*, in which investment hucksters target a group of people with shared background, age, or interests, such as religious or ethnic affiliations. Affinity fraud often incorporates Ponzi schemes and other types of bogus investments as the actual vehicles for stealing "investors'" money. The SEC website (investor.gov) gives a number of examples of illegal business schemes based in affinity fraud. One of those examples outlines a scheme in which a promoter targeted members of an African-American church-going community.[44] The promoter sold these investors promissory notes with rates of 12% to 20%, saying that the notes would be used to fund small businesses. Of course, the money went straight into the pocket of the promoter. Another scheme noted on the SEC website involved members of the Cuban exile population in Florida, who were sold real-estate "investments" in a classic Ponzi scheme that simply paid old investors with new investors' money.[45]

Our good friend Bernard Madoff also made use of affinity fraud. He rarely promoted his own "investments," instead relying on word of mouth among his growing list of high-profile clients. After conning members of the general public for his Ponzi scheme, he began targeting his own religious and social group, which included a number of wealthy Jewish people from the country club set in New York, Hollywood and Palm Beach. When the big money there began to dry up, he switched it up to charitable foundations, which turned out to be a very safe and profitable group to bilk. Why? Because they have to give away 5% of their assets yearly, but typically don't try to take out all of their investment profits at once.

And Madoff wouldn't swindle just anyone; his marks had to be recommended to him by other marks and, like Charles Ponzi, he often wouldn't even talk to a potential customer. If you asked too many questions, Madoff gave you your money back or wouldn't let you invest in the first place. Once you got out, you couldn't get back in. Perhaps the most brilliant and creative part of his swindle is that he never promised outrageous returns, just a stunningly steady 10% or 12% a year, even in down markets, which lulled investors into thinking their investment was safe and smart. Many of his victims thought it was a privilege to be invested with Madoff, and they boasted of it to others, some of whom then also wanted to invest. As this swindler demonstrated so clearly, anyone can fall victim to affinity fraud scams. We trust our friends and associates, and we certainly believe that major organizations aren't going to be victims of a swindle. So, when those investors fall for a con artist, we're likely to follow them down the rabbit hole.

Victor's Advice

Affinity fraud can be hard to prove and prosecute, because victims often are ashamed of being scammed and reluctant to blow the lid off of a scam being participated in (if not perpetrated by) friends and associates. As in all of life, avoiding the problem can be much easier than fixing it. Here are four tips from Freddie Mac for avoiding affinity fraud[46]:

1. **Do your research:** Don't take anyone's word for anything when it comes to investing. Before putting in one thin dime, investigate the person offering the investment opportunity, as well as the opportunity itself. If you're dealing with a friend, get an outside financial expert's advice on the deal.

2. **Don't assume people are honest:** Recommendations alone aren't a basis for jumping into any investment. Doesn't matter if the person making the recommendation is a good friend, a casual acquaintance, or a total stranger, verify, verify, verify. Go online, talk to other investors, and get that independent third-party input.

3. **If it sounds too good to be true...you know the rest:** No real investment is total risk free. If an opportunity is sold to you as having no risk and paying unbelievably high returns, fast, walk away—fast.

4. **Get it in writing and suspect any attempt at secrecy:** Most affinity fraudsters don't want to put their deals in writing, and they often ask you to keep the investment hush-hush. Either of those conditions is a red flag that fraud is in the air. Don't buy into it.

Pump and Dump Schemes: The Can't-Lose Deal that Does

When I was a relatively new investor, I bought stock in a gold mining company which was recommended by my stockbroker and a number of articles in investment newsletters. The stock was priced at $1.10 a share, which I felt offered a can't-lose deal, since my sources were recommending the stock. I was excited when the stock went up to $1.15 a share, but then watched in burning dismay as its price rapidly dropped to 25 cents. Biting back my embarrassment, I sold after losing 75% of my investment. At the time, I didn't know what hit me. It was only years later that I realized that I may have been the victim of a *pump and dump* scheme. I believe now that a group of unscrupulous insiders and traders had bought up a lot of the stock for pennies a share, then recommended and promoted the stock to unsuspecting investors such as myself. When our purchases pumped up the stock's value, the insiders dumped their shares, and the sell-off plummeted the stock's value to next to nothing.

As you begin investing for the future, you can expect to occasionally get calls, emails, or offers via social media to buy small company stocks at relatively low per-share prices. Don't take the bait. There are several problems with these deals. First, small companies aren't well–traded, so you may have difficulty finding a buyer when you go to sell. More importantly, though, their stock prices can fluctuate dramatically based on new sales. While McDonald's or IBM have to sell millions of shares to shift their stock's per-share price, it doesn't take much to drive up (or down) the value of a small company's stock. You and a few other "new investors" can quickly run up the stock's initial sale price, giving insider traders a great opportunity to dump their shares and collect their profits. When the hypesters sell off their shares and stop flogging the stock, you're left holding the (very empty) bag.

Typically, the pitch for a pump and dump scheme is that you're being offered a "can't lose" deal, but you have to act immediately while the stock is still at a "bargain rate." Latent greed kicks in, maybe accompanied by a big dose of hubris, and we go for it. Back in Chapter 2 we talked about Regret Aversion, in which our fear of losing out on a great deal overwhelms our ability to understand that the deal is, in fact, a lousy investment. That kind of behavioral investing is what keeps pump and dump schemes alive and well in today's marketplace.

Getting Help for Saying NO

So, are we all doomed to get taken down by scam artists and their ever-evolving schemes? Not necessarily. While it's true that scam artists never seem to run out of willing victims, there's no reason that we have to be among them. By keeping our eyes open and our greed in check, we can learn to spot the "too-good-to-be-true" deals and "you-can-trust-me" thieves who offer them long before they get close enough to our money to grab it and run. And, if we know where to look for it, there's help out there available for any of us who has trouble knowing when and where and with whom we should invest.

As you have probably assumed by this point, the Internet can be a friend to scam artists—and a big problem for the rest of us. Whether they're selling stocks in bogus companies or making offers to bring you into Ponzi or pyramid schemes, affinity frauds, pump and dump operations, or any other type of investment scam, first contact by email or social media is a favored approach for fraudsters. First, it's virtually costless to send you an email. Secondly, the Internet offers these crooks digital camouflage, as they never have to show you their face or credentials. Spammers get addresses by scanning the web using proprietary software, by buying lists from reputable organizations, and even by merely guessing at viable addresses. If you haven't already received bogus investment offers via email or online, you will. Often, the very wording of these communications reveals them to be the work of people who aren't working for established, legitimate businesses. Gross errors in spelling or grammar, outlandish claims and promises, and weirdly convoluted explanations are just some of the giveaways in these bogus offers.

Victor's Advice

I'm sorry to say that in reality, almost all of the unsolicited emails you get to buy goods or services are suspect. That means you need to have a great spam blocker in your email program. You also have to discipline yourself to deal exclusively with sites that have a well-documented reputation for honesty and quality—then delete email or unsolicited offers via social media that manage to squeak through your blocker.

Not all scams and frauds come to us digitally, of course. The SEC (Securities and Exchange Commission) is our government's agency tasked with tracking, reporting on, and exposing investment scams and schemes. The organization has its hands full, as you can imagine. The SEC documents its ongoing activities and findings on its website (www.investor.gov), and the agency has done a good job of organizing that information for the benefit of everyday citizens like you and me. There, you can read up on various types of fraudulent investment schemes and recent activity in each of them. The site also publishes ongoing Investor Alerts to shed light on new schemes as they emerge. Here's a brief list of ideas the experts at the SEC offer for recognizing and avoiding investment scams and schemes:

- **Consider suspect all unsolicited offers to invest.** Reputable brokers and firms don't fish in unknown waters for investors. Any unsolicited offer that comes via email, a social media site, or through casual personal/business associates should raise a red flag.
- **Don't say "yes" without doing your own investigation.** Scammers have no reason to give you honest information about their 'enterprises.' Do your own independent investigation into the organization, its representatives, and its products and/or processes before you invest.
- **Check the broker's licensing, registration, and reputation.** Don't hand over investment money to someone just because they belong to your country club, go to your place of worship, or are a member of your alumni association. Make sure a broker is licensed to sell securities in your state by checking with your state's securities regulator. The Investment Advisor section of the SEC's site (SEC.gov) is worth examining, as is

www.brokercheck.org, a site created and managed by the
Financial Industry Regulatory Authority (FINRA), to check the
disciplinary history and background of any broker or
brokerage firm.

- **Be wary of online investment "newsletters," opinion
  research, and spam mailings.** It's not unusual for scammers to
  put together an online letter or publication that appears to be
  gathering opinions on or offering 'expert' insights into
  investment schemes that, in truth, are pure frauds. Again, do
  your research before returning information or following
  advice asked for or offered by unsolicited/unknown sources—
  even when they advertise on the pages of well-known news
  organizations.
- **Resist the "you must act now" pitch.** Good investments never
  need to happen in a hurry. If someone tries to pressure you to
  jump on a good deal, back away instead.
- **Let the bandwagon pass you by.** When someone, whether a
  promoter you've just met or a member of your social circle,
  tells you that 'everyone is getting in' on a deal, assume the
  deal isn't for you. You're more interested in the quality of the
  stock, fund, or company you're backing than in how many
  people are buying into it.

One final piece of advice I can offer you is this: Don't shut up out of
shame. If you think you have become the victim of—or have even been
approached by—an investment scammer or shady investment
organization, don't refuse to speak up because you feel embarrassed.
Instead, contact someone who can help you get to the bottom of the
situation. You can turn to the SEC, FINRA, or your state securities
regulator to get help.[47]

Avoiding Risky Financial Advisors

If I've convinced you of anything in the first six chapters of this book, I
hope it's that managing finances and financial investments can be quite

complicated. That's why so many people are happy to turn over the task to professional financial advisors. And that's not a bad idea; most financial advisors are honest and capable. They can help you review your finances, establish a budget, set goals for your investments, and make a plan for achieving those goals. Most importantly, they can guide you in sticking with that plan, and making changes to it as necessary. But, you can't hand over the keys to your financial future to just anyone. Instead, when choosing an advisor, you have to do your due diligence, so you know who you are trusting with your money, and what qualifications they have for earning that trust.

Don't worry, though; you aren't left to wander around in the dark as you look for the best person to guide your finances. In fact, there are multiple certifications within the field of financial advising, and they can be useful tools for identifying advisors who have achieved certain standards within the industry. Here are a few of the more important certifications you should look for in anyone you're considering as a financial advisor:

- **Certified Financial Planner-**Only the most well-trained and experienced financial advisors achieve CFP® certification. Applicants for this certification must take a series of courses covering financial aspects of insurance, retirement and estate planning, and investing. They then have to pass a day-long examination of their knowledge in the field and prove that they've accomplished a proscribed length and type of experience in order to receive the certification.
- **Chartered Financial Consultant-**The ChFC or Chartered Financial Consultant certification requires the same core coursework as the CFP® certification, along with a few additional courses aimed at expanding the applicant's training in personal financial planning.[48] Neither has a significant educational prerequisite according to the American College of Financial Services web site.

- **Charted Financial Analyst-**A CFA, or chartered financial analyst, receives perhaps the most academically rigorous coursework of any financial advisor certification program. All applicants
- must have a college degree to be considered for the program. Then, they have to complete certification program training to develop expertise in financial and security analysis, economics, and investment management. Most of the "charter" holders as they are called end up as mutual fund managers or financial analysts; only a small percentage become financial advisors. The CFA is the most prestigious of the financial certifications, and you may have a hard time finding one to be your financial advisor, as they can have a much more challenging and lucrative career working for large financial institutions.
- **Chartered Life Underwriter-**CLU or Chartered Life Underwriter certification indicates that the bearer is knowledgeable about life insurance. While most CLUs are associated with the insurance industry, some specialize in estate planning. Applicants have to take a proscribed set of courses and pass a series of examinations to receive this certification.
- **Broker or Registered Representative-**Brokers, more accurately called Registered Representatives, are financial professionals who are allowed to recommend, buy, and sell securities and mutual funds for clients. Registered representatives have to pass a qualifying examination, register with FINRA (the Financial Institutions Regulatory Authority), and be licensed by the securities regulator in the state in which they're operating.[49] Registered representatives are required to make suitable buy and sell recommendations to clients, based on the clients' income, other investment holdings, risk tolerance, and other factors. They are not, however, required to represent their clients' best interests.
- **Registered Investment Advisor-**A Registered Investment Advisor, or RIA, can be either an individual or a firm that offers investment advice. For an individual to certified as an RIA,

applicants must take a qualifying examination and be registered with the SEC or with the state securities authorities.

- **Registered Financial Consultant-**Another certification program for registered representatives and other financial advisors. To earn RFC certification, applicants must have any one of fifteen qualifying degrees or certifications, or complete an approved college curriculum. They also must meet the RFC licensing and experience requirements.

This list doesn't cover all of the many types of certifications, acronyms, and areas of specialization for financial advisors, but it does cover those you're most likely to encounter. In reviewing the knowledge qualifications for these certifications, I found that those required for the CFP® and CFA seem to be the most rigorous. But knowledge doesn't necessarily translate into skill, and neither knowledge nor skill guarantee honesty.

That's why it's important that you do a little background research on any financial advisor you're considering. Don't dismiss the importance of checking into the background of a potential advisor. FINRA's brokercheck website will not only give you information about a broker's certifications, tests, and previous employment, it also records complaints and actions that have been lodged against the broker. Remember, you don't have to rely on your "gut feel" about a broker or take someone's word about the broker's qualifications and honesty. Well-documented information is out there to help you learn more about anyone you're considering as a financial advisor or money manager. Use it!

Victor's Advice

Brokers don't have to be out-and-out crooks to cost you money—or to trigger client complaints--so it pays to check the history of *every* broker, financial advisor, or consultant you engage with. Years ago, I had a financial advisor who was college educated with an advanced degree in finance. He was a nice guy, but the investments he sold me never outperformed the S&P 500, which I could have invested in on my own (and without his fees). I decided to try a little experiment. I invested equal sums with him and with a Vanguard fund in the S&P 500. After three years, the advisor's investments hadn't done any better than mine, so I left his firm. Recently, I decided to check his complaint history on brokercheck, and it wasn't pretty. This guy has had multiple complaints about his services over the years, two of which ended in settlements. Had I spent some time checking on him *before* I invested with his firm, I might have avoided him altogether and the opportunity costs of tying up my money in his lackluster investment picks. Learn from my mistake, do some research, and save yourself the time and money I wasted on a go-nowhere (or, even worse, dishonest) financial advisor.

Recognizing Your Risk for Being Scammed

So, we've seen that there are plenty of ways to fall into the clutches of investment scams and schemers. From Ponzi and pyramid scams, to affinity fraud, pump and dump schemes, and shady (or merely ineffective) financial advisors, the options for being ripped off as an investor are many and constantly multiplying. And who are the most common victims of these bad deals and dealers? As I hope the information in this chapter makes clear, we—you and I and just about everyone we know—are the targets investment scammers have in their sites.

I can't stress that fact enough, because it's so very easy to believe we're too smart to be caught in a scam artist's web. For much of my life, I would have said that the folks who got tangled in investment schemes were probably young, uneducated, and financially unsophisticated. Wow, was I wrong! While *anyone* can fall victim to a scam, some of us seem to be more likely to take the bait. According to Stanford University psychologist, Laura Carstenson, co-founder of the Financial Fraud

Research Center, the typical financial fraud victim is a "middle-aged, educated, financially literate white male" who, in many cases, is dealing with financial difficulties.[50]

That fits with what I know now about the folks who are most susceptible to investment scams. My personal experience and observation also have taught me that the perfect victim is likely to be a bit greedy and willing to take big risks to win big. Sadly, even experiencing a tragedy such as divorce, death in the family, or a large financial hit can put us squarely in the crosshairs of someone gunning for our financial resources.

How closely do you fit the profile of a typical victim of investment fraud? While it's by no means all-inclusive, here's a list from FINRA of the five factors that most often put people at risk of falling victim to an investment scam:[51]

1. Owning high-risk investments, such as penny stocks, promissory notes, futures, and so on.
2. Relying on friends, family, and co-workers for financial advice.
3. Being open to investment information from unfamiliar sources, such as from a free investment seminar.
4. Failing to check a broker's background, licensing, and registration.
5. Failing to spot high-pressure tactics and subtle pressure from scammers, such as being urged to act immediately or to recruit others to participate in an investment.

You can do more to fill in your own risk for being a victim of financial fraud by using FINRA's Risk Meter, at finra.org, or by taking the AARP (American Association of Retired Persons) investment fraud vulnerability quiz at www.aarp.org.

Money is important to everyone, but those of us who have a higher-than-average income have to invest if we want our money to work for us and last throughout our lifetime. That means we're often ready to listen to investment ideas, whether they come from known and trusted sources, or just seem to drop in our lap. Telephone solicitations, social media contacts, business mailings, even that invitation to a free dinner-- scams can take many forms and leverage any means of contact with out-of-the blue offers that "can't lose" as long as we "act NOW!" It's on us to keep our heads and make smart decisions when one of these crooks comes calling. Some of us will do just that, but many others will take the bait and get hooked into a scam.

It's only natural to want to believe that our common sense and investment savvy can help us make a haul in the stock market. We *want* to be part of big, bold ideas and pioneering opportunities to make a fortune that everyone else has overlooked. Unfortunately, while those opportunities do occasionally arise, it takes a lot of money, a lot of time, and finely-honed skills in investment management to recognize and participate profitably in them. Hush-hush deals and under-the-radar investment advice aren't tickets to great fortune. More often, they're invitations to a rip-off.

In essence, I think that avoiding scams demands a type of maturity that, while not great for landing us in exciting adventures, is absolutely essential for avoiding the catastrophic financial losses and confidence- shaking humiliation of being a victim of a scam. When I was young, I relied on my innate intuition to spot a good deal. I also thought I had the money, time, and experience to play with the big dogs, make bold and unconventional financial moves, and quickly build a fortune. The passing years have disabused me of those laughable notions. I now know that finding solid investment vehicles and avoiding scams and bad deals isn't a matter of boldness, strong "gut sense," and inherent financial savvy. Nope, building wealth isn't about piracy, it's about planning, research, and patience. It also demands that we master the single most important skill for avoiding bad investments and keeping our money out of the hands of scam artists: We have to learn to say NO!

CHAPTER 7: SAYING NO TO HIGH FEES AND EXPENSIVE ADVICE

You've decided to finally start investing on a regular basis, and you're considering whether or not to find a good financial advisor. You're a good 30 years from retirement, so you have some time to build a solid investment portfolio that will provide for your financial needs long after you've stopped working. You do some preliminary research and become convinced that your best bet is to start investing monthly in a solid index fund. You also schedule a preliminary interview with a financial advisor who has been recommended by one of your friends. She tells you that index funds aren't a bad idea, but you'll still need to work with a professional to make sure that your portfolio remains balanced between stock and bond index funds and up-to-date with changing market conditions. She also states that her charges are approximately 1.25%. You want the advice--you're new to investing and this woman seems knowledgeable and trustworthy. Should you sign with this advisor?

Answer: NO!

First, you're on the right track with your research, but you need to do a bit more. Yes, you may benefit from working with an advisor when you're new to investing. And that's true even if you decide to buy and hold index funds. Saving for retirement is rarely a "one and done" process, so having someone to advise you, help in your selections, and recommend periodic portfolio tweaking can be a sound decision. But you have no idea whether this advisor—and her rate—are the right choice. In my opinion, anything over 0.75% is too much. You can check out this woman's credentials and history through the Investment Advisor section of the SEC.gov site and at brokercheck.com. Then, make sure you find out how this advisor views her role progressing over the years, and ask her specifically what services she intends to provide to you throughout your investment career. Finally, meet with a few other candidates, ask them the same questions, and make a decision when you're better informed about what an advisor can do for you and how much those services should cost.

We've spent a lot of time in this book talking about how to say NO to questionable investment opportunities, and we've even talked about learning to spot and say NO to a questionable financial advisor. But it's just as important to learn to say NO to questionable investment *fees.* By that, I mean the excessive fees charged by some investment advisors and mutual funds. According to the Bureau of Labor Statistics more than 6 million Americans are financial services professionals, and more than 330,000 of them are involved directly with the investment industry. So, we should have no problem finding someone to give us financial advice. That advice costs, of course, so it's up to us to make sure that the advice we're getting is worth its price.

Here's a simple example that illustrates how mutual fund fees can add up. According to Morningstar, the average mutual fund fee (at the time of this writing) was 1.25% per year, which amounts to around $75 a year on a $6000 investment. New investors, in particular, look at that amount and shrug—it's no big deal, right? But, over time, that simple fee can add up to a substantial amount of money. Let's say you're 25 years old and you've just started putting $500 a month in an IRA. As an example, we offer later in this chapter illustrates, by the time you're ready to retire, that 1.25% fee could have cost you almost $1,205,069! Now, *that* fee charge seems like a much bigger deal, doesn't it? And, let's not forget about the opportunity costs of fees, as well. All in all, even small fees can add up to a big expense.

In Chapter 6 we reviewed the types of financial/investment advisors you can choose from and the ways they charge for their services. In this chapter, we focus our attention on typical fees for investments, who charges the fees, and what they pay for. Clearing the fog from fee charges isn't as simple as it may sound. Many investments can rack up more than one fee; you may pay your broker or advisor's fee, plus a shareholder fee, an exchange fee, purchase fee, redemption fee, and others, that cover the basic costs of management, operation, administration of the fund you've invested in. Those added fees can dramatically drive up the cost of owning mutual funds. A 2011 article from *Forbes* online estimated that the true cost of owning a mutual fund was really more like 3.17% for non-taxable accounts and a whopping 4.17% for taxable accounts.[52]

Sorting through all of these fees and costs can be a difficult process, and I think that's why so many investors simply throw their hands in the air and agree to pay "whatever it takes" to make their investments grow. That's a mistake. Yes, there are some perfectly legitimate reasons for working with an investment advisor or broker. But that decision should be a thoughtful one, based on your clear understanding of how much involvement you want to have in managing your investments, what an advisor can do for you, what a reasonable charge for those services should be—and how willing you are to cut into your returns in order to pay that cost. You'll be on solid ground for making those calls after you've stepped through the information in this chapter.

Here, we'll overview some of the typical fees and expenses charged by funds (including those that can go beyond "reasonable") and how much of a chunk they can carve out of your investment return. We'll get to the bottom of wrap fees, 12b-1 fees, and some other sometimes obscure and potentially overpriced fees, and we'll outline simple information that can help you deflate the pressure of an investment advisor's sales pitch. We'll even talk about how to mine the mighty mass of a fund's prospectus to find the tiny gem of information you actually need to know in order to make a sound investment decision. In the process, we'll step through the amazingly simple process for finding low-fee funds that offer solid returns while saving you money on fees and expenses.

Remember, this book is aimed at making you rich, but it's not a ticket to overnight fortune. Becoming rich through investment is a long-term process. And over the twenty or thirty or more years that you'll be building wealth for retirement, even the smallest fees can add up to a sizeable portion of your investment assets. That's why learning to say NO to unnecessarily expensive fees and advice is as important to your investment success as rejecting offers to invest in risky businesses and getting real about your ability to time the market. When the goal is to use our investments to become rich, we can't afford to be pushovers when it comes to paying fees.

Victor's Advice

What are the three biggest culprits when it comes to eroding investor returns? Investor behavior (take a look back at Chapter 2 for more on that), attempts to time the market, and unreasonable fees. Fortunately, you don't have to let any of these factors eat away at your investment returns. Know and control your behavioral investing impulses, forget about finding a magical formula for jumping in and out of the market, and learn what fees are reasonable and necessary for your investment processes and goals. If you can do those three things, you'll be miles ahead of many individual investors in today's marketplace.

As you read this chapter, bear in mind that I'm not advising you on how or when to make any particular type of investment in any specific fund or company. I use various funds to illustrate the chapter's information, but those examples are for explanation only. The advice I offer here is strictly informational, and I don't intend it as specific investment advice. My goal for offering my advice here is to better equip you to make your *own* decisions about choosing investments or hiring an advisor to help you in that process.

Taking a First Look at Fees

Let me make a confession right up front: There's no way I can make the information about fees sexy. I'll try not to put you into a reader's coma here, but to keep the investment fees you pay to a minimum, you need to have an understanding of how the fees work. Most of the new investors I work with are worried about losing their money to a stock market crash or bond blow-up, but honestly, that shouldn't be an investor's biggest worry. Those debacles might happen, or they might not. You are *certain* to lose money, though, if you pay excessive fees for your investments.

Finding a good mutual fund or other investment vehicle that will work for *your* interests, *your* finances, *your* goals can be an overwhelming process. The system for finding, making, and managing investments is complex and made even more opaque and confusing by the investment industry itself. Why should they make it easier for you to do work that they would like to do—for a hefty fee? So, it's easy to understand why so many people end up turning over the task to a financial advisor or broker. As we saw in Chapter 6, investment advisors come in many different varieties, and their charges can be just as variable. A lot of that variability results from the fees charged by the funds and other investments they're selling.

Just like everyone else, investment advisors have to be paid by someone, in some way. I always recommend working with an advisor who you pay directly for their time and service, rather than turning your investment finances over to someone who gets paid a commission for recommending a specific stock or mutual fund. Still, there are good, solid reasons that some investors wisely choose to pay for some types of advice and trading services. Remember, there's no free lunch when financial investments are on the table. That's why almost all funds charge some form of *expense ratio,* an annual fee funds use to cover the cost of operation, management, administration, and so on. Those charges typically run between a low of 0.03% of the investment total for an S&P 500 Index fund, to as much as 1.50% for a foreign stock fund.[53]

Victor's Advice

Mutual fund fees have been on a downward trend for years, and that's probably going to continue. With index funds turning in great performance with minimal management and fees, fewer investors are willing to fork over high fees for funds that can't really beat the index. If a fund is charging more than 1% total for all services related to the fund, I advise you to look elsewhere for a good long-term investment.

Figure 7.1 shows a summary of the various fees charged by mutual funds and their advisors, and it includes fees you pay with each transaction as well as those you pay on an annual basis. Some fees are legitimate charges necessary to cover the costs of doing business. Other charges have no real basis in a "service" provided to or for investors but are simply padding that investment companies use to boost their profits. In my opinion, the only legitimate fee any fund should charge is for management, and management fees typically are included in the fund's expense ratio. When you see a long list of other fees and charges associated with a fund, you can assume those fees aren't going to benefit shareholders by improving their investment results. Instead, they may be paying for things like the advertisement and promotion of the company's products—or, maybe for the brokers' and advisors' football tickets and company Christmas party.

Figure 7.1: Common Transactional and Ongoing Fees for Mutual Funds

Transaction Fees	Ongoing Fees
Mutual Fund Loads	Management Fees
Back End Load	Custodial Fees
Reinvestment Fee	401(k) fees
Stock Trading Fee	Wrap Fees
Bid-ask spreads	12b-1 Fees
Account Transfer Fees	
Account inactivity Fee	
Low Balance Fee	
Wire Transfer Fee	Annual Variable Annuity Fees

Consider for example the 12b-1 fee, perhaps the most anti-investor, pro-financial industry fee of all. An SEC (Securities and Exchange Commission) rule based on legislation that dates back to the 1940s allows a fund to charge shareholders an annual 12b-1 fee of as much as 1.00% of the value of their shares, for advertising and promotion and some shareholder services. The money from the 12b-1 fee may be used to compensate broker/advisors for sales of their funds, as well as for shareholder expenses such as prospectuses and sales literature. FINRA (the Financial Industry Regulatory Authority) limits the marketing and distribution fees to 0.75% or 75 basis points of the average net assets of the mutual fund and caps the service fees at 0.25% (25 basis points).

Note that not one red penny of that money goes to doing research on fund investments or to increase the return on shareholder investments.

The 12b-1 fee is just one example of the costs associated with buying and selling some mutual funds. And, again, while these fees may seem inconsequential or simply the cost of doing business, they actually matter a lot. They grow exponentially over the years, as does their opportunity cost. Figure 7.2 illustrates just how the cost of fees paid over the lifetime of an investment can severely eat into the investment's returns.

FIGURE 7.2: EROSION OF INVESTMENT RETURNS FROM FEES

In plain dollars and cents, Figure 7.3 shows how fees of 1.25% and 0.04% erode returns on an investment funded by a $500-per-month IRA contribution. This table assumes successive increases in the contribution amount to account for inflation and a 10% yearly return, which is the average rate of return for the S&P 500 Index over many years.

FIGURE 7.3: A COMPARISON OF RETURNS OVER 40 YEARS, BASED ON FEES OF 1.25% AND 0.04%

	INDEX	0.04% Fee	1.25% Fee	Difference Index and 0.04%	Difference Index-1.25% fee
20 YEARS	$464,017	$461,628	$394,396	$2,389	$69,621
25 YEARS	$824,145	$818,715	$668,721	$5,429	$155,424
30 YEARS	$1,416,373	$1,404,883	$1,094,292	$11,490	$322,081
40 YEARS	$3,959,738	$3,914,695	$2,754,668	$45,042	$1,205,069

In this comparison, the first column shows the returns we would receive if we were lucky enough to find an index fund that charged absolutely no fees at all. That won't happen, but I've included the returns in this column to highlight just how much of our investment is going toward the fees charged by the other two funds in this example. At 25 years, our return is dinged a total of $155,424 by the 1.25% fee fund, and $5429 by the lower 0.04% fee fund. At 40 years, we're paying the lower-fee fund $45,042 and a stunning $1,205,069 to the higher-fee fund! Now that's what fees and expenses can do to you.

So, let's take a closer look at just a few of these fees and the types of funds that charge them, so you can make an informed decision about which funds work best in your long-range plan to build wealth.

Carrying the Load, or Going It Alone

Let's begin to clear away the fog of investment fees by looking at some of the simplest examples, fund loads. A *load* is a transaction fee that investors pay for buying or selling a particular mutual fund. Funds that charge those fees are called *load funds*; those that don't are called *no-load funds*. You might pay a *front-end* load when you buy a load fund, or you might pay a *back-end* load or *contingent deferred sales charge* (CDSC) when you sell it. Investment companies such as the American

Funds, Dreyfus, PIMCO, Templeton and many others have some funds that pay fees back to brokers and advisors and their companies. These are commission payments that you can think of as sales charges. If the mutual fund charges operational expenses, typically the charge is included in the expense ratio, which does *not* include any load the fund also may charge. Other investment companies, including T. Rowe Price and Vanguard, have no-load funds that charge very few fees of a modest amount.

Victor's Advice

The load fee is supposed to pay for the research and trading necessary to research advice and trading when you buy and sell a fund. You may want to use an advisor to make those decisions, or you may opt to take on the research necessary to make an informed decision about buying or selling a mutual fund, along with the transaction process itself. If you don't want to work with an advisor, there's no reason for you to buy a load fund.

In most cases, load charges are associated with the type or *class* of funds shareholders are buying. While *stock share classes* have to do with the individual company and the voting rights it assigns to its shareholders, *mutual fund classes* are used to designate how shareholders pay for their investment. Here's a quick overview of the most common mutual fund classes and types. Remember, these are just broad descriptions of the mutual fund classes, not endorsements or advice for buying them:

- **Class A:** "A" shares typically have a front-end load of up to 5.00%.[54] For example, if you buy $5000 worth of "A" shares, and the load fee is 5%, $250 of your upfront money goes to the advisor or broker and their company and you have $4750 actually invested in the fund. Some funds offer discounts for higher levels of investment, called *breakpoint discounts*. Those discounts often attract investors who are investing really large amounts of money for a very long time.

- **Class B:** "B" shares typically charge a back-end load or CDSC of as much as 5% to investors when they sell their shares. These funds sometimes have a larger annual management fee (the 12b-1 fee, which is included as part of the expense ratio) and they may not offer breakpoint discounts. Over time, the CDSC may decrease, however, and take the fees with it. Check the individual Class B share details to determine whether the fees and share status change over time.

- **Class C:** "C" shares are also sometimes known as *level-load* shares because they carry an annual fee that stays the same for as long as you own the shares. These fees typically are around 1% of the total investment, but because they last throughout the time you own the shares, they can be a big drag on the returns you receive as an investor and may cost you more than Class A or B shares in the long run.

- **Class R:** "R" shares typically are linked to retirement funds. Most don't charge a load, but they may include 12b-1 fees. You might have these shares in a 401k.

- **Class T:** "T" shares are a relatively recent type of mutual fund shares, introduced by the industry in response to fiduciary rule (more on that later). T shares differ from A, B and C shares in that fund companies selling the shares charge the same load price across all funds, to eliminate the temptation for a broker or advisor to advise a client to buy a particular fund in order to earn a higher commission. The front-end load for T shares may be 2.5% (larger purchases may have a lower load), and they also may carry a 0.25% 12b-1 fee.[55]

- **Investor shares:** Investor shares are those that are purchased by individuals rather than large organizations or institutions. These investments typically have higher fees, but the total amount of the investment account can be quite small, for example just a few thousand dollars. In comparison, at the time of this writing the Vanguard Admiral shares require accounts to hold at least $10,000 but charge much lower management fees.

Index funds, as we've seen, are long-term investment vehicles that require very little maintenance. Why is that? First, you do not have to pay an investment manager to do research and make any investment decisions. The index is bought and sold based on the value of the component companies. For example, as of this book's publication, the largest US company, Apple represented 3.6%[56] of the value of the Standard and Poor's 500 index with Microsoft a close second at 3% whereas the significant increase in the value of Amazon stock propelled the company into third place at 2.5%. Facebook, which was not even in the index until a few years ago is fourth at 1.83%. When you invest $100 in the index, $3.60 goes into Apple stock while almost $11.00 goes into purchasing the previously mentioned top four. Of course, when you go to sell your index, you sell in relatively the same proportions depending on the price and value of the underlying stocks. Here is the beauty of an index, companies move up and down depending on how the market values their goods and services. Sears and Eastman Kodak are no longer in the index, and you never had to make a decision to sell nor did you need to make a decision when to buy Facebook. You buy an index funds leave them alone for years at a time while they, if all goes well, continue to gain value. These aren't funds that demand investors to engage in frequent decision-making or trading, so investing in these funds doesn't require a lot of hand-holding advice or guidance—and they typically have very low management fees or expense ratios. But even some index funds charge loads, so you have to watch carefully to avoid paying a load fee for advice and transaction help that you don't want and aren't getting.

Overall, your investment results from A or B shares may be lower than those you would have had with a no-load index fund. When you're turning over all of these fees and fund classes in your mind, though, remember that their status can change over time, as with "B" shares that lose their back-end load over time and transfer to "A" shares. Many people may get the equivalent of "A" shares, for example, when they buy "R" class shares in funds through their work place. Employers can negotiate to get "R" shares from the same mutual fund issuing "A" shares, so their employees can avoid the load. I was able to get "R" shares in the American AMCAP (RAFGX) fund through my workplace, for example, and eventually the shares were converted to A shares. So, I ended up with a front-end load fund that I didn't have to pay a load fee for. Pretty sweet!

Victor's Advice

While the 12b-1 fee is limited to 1% of total fund assets by FINRA, the amount companies charge for this fee typically differs by stock class. Stocks that carry a load, essentially Class A and B stocks, may charge a reduced 12b-1 fee. Class C stocks are more likely to charge the full 1% 12b-1 since they usually don't charge load fees.

Avoiding the Trap of the Wrap

Loads and 12b-1 fees aren't the only culprits when it comes to eating away at your investment returns. You also have to be on the lookout for *wrap fees,* the annual fee paid to a financial broker or advisor for a whole range of services, including advice, research, and more. The fee, which typically replaces front-end and back-end loads, usually works out to about 0.05% to 2% of the total amount of assets in the investment, which sounds reasonable to many investors. But lots of investors in mutual funds don't realize that the wrap fee goes only to the broker/advisor; it doesn't cover any of the fund's management fees. When we tack on those costs, now we're paying maybe 2% to 3% in annual fees, thanks to the wrap.

I have an associate who decided to pay into a wrap account to manage her 401(K). For 1.3% of her 401(K) assets, her advising company bought a series of mutual funds which included stock and bond funds. With much trading, her account made 6% returns in a year when the comparable indices were up 12%. Why was that? First, she was paying

1.3% a year for "advice" which just may have been the results of a computer program analysis and trading. On top of that, the majority of the funds purchased on this advice had management and 12b-1 fees. So, she may have been paying as much as 2.5% or more for this "management!" Logically, we could assume that the funds she bought paid higher returns than the comparable index funds—but they didn't. So, my associate paid more and received much less than she could have from her retirement investments.

When I asked her investment "advisor" what the problem was, he said, "Well, people would rather not see their assets go down, so they pay a price for being safe." A 6% loss in returns makes for a pretty expensive safety measure if you ask me. The same thing happened to my father-in-law. His investment advisor did so much trading in 1998 that every few days, my father-in-law was getting a trade confirmation in the mail. He was paying a wrap fee and getting well-below-market returns of around 5%, when the comparable stock and bond markets were up 22%. So, that's the great advice and service my father-in-law got for the price of his wrap fee. The take-away here is pretty simple: We always need to cut the fees we pay to a minimum and make as much money as we can get when the markets are going up. That way, we can weather the storm when they hit a down draft.

Should You Say YES or NO? Seeing Through the Sales Pitch

Investment sales people like to tell you that they can make up for many of the fees charged by the funds they are selling you over time because their managers are better at buying and selling at the right times in the market. And, that can be true. At the same time, are you really going to benefit from all of that trade activity? In any given year, 75% of funds fail to beat the returns achieved by comparable index funds (or the market average without fees). Part of the reason for that is because of fees and costs, but the other part is the result of manager investment error.

To compensate, or at least minimize, the hit our investments will take as a result of paying advisory and load fees, investors have to find a fund that is actually going to *beat* what the market does in price appreciation—and it has to beat the market not just one year, but for many years over a long period of time. Finding that fund can be a very difficult task, one that I certainly feel incapable of, even with my MBA, investment experience, and a lot of available time and interest. In fact, the odds of landing such a fund are so slim that it's not worth the opportunity cost of the effort involved. Maybe the advisor you're talking to can do that, but you need to see proof of that in the form of past results. Don't take it on faith—or empty promises—that an advisor can find and manage funds for you that will "earn away" the fees.

Victor's Advice

You should be aware that if your advisor or fund manager becomes known for beating the market, she's likely to be moved out of the low-level advising business (where compensation is relatively low, as well) and on to managing large portfolios where there's real money to be made. In this system, small investors almost never win.

But that's not to say that there aren't good reasons for deciding to pay reasonable fees, so you can have the help of an investment advisor. Maybe you don't want to spend the time doing the research necessary to choose the right fund for your investment needs, or maybe you don't have the time or the inclination to do so. Maybe you want a calm third-party advisor who can keep you from making rash decisions about buying and selling as the market changes over time. Many successful market analysts will tell you that making good investment decisions is as much about sound judgment as it is about long-term experience. I'd say the same is true about deciding whether or not to go it alone in your investment adventures. Think about your personality, your interests, your time demands; if all of them fit with the process of buying and managing your own portfolio, you can save some serious money on fees. If you don't want to take on that job (or don't feel up to it), you can always pay the fees and sleep easier at night. In that case, though, you still need to carefully review *all* of the fees being charged by the fund or advisor you're considering and make an informed decision about whether the services you're going to be paying for are worth the load you'll carry. As I've said before, if the annual fees add up to more than 0.75% of your total investment, you need to think carefully about how the fees will add up over the years and why you'd want to give up that much of your wealth.

When we buy a car, we pretty much know the markup and profit being made by the dealer, because those figures are published and (usually) even posted right there on the car's windshield. The investment industry isn't that transparent. And, the industry is so replete with fees and costs that may occur over time, that it becomes very difficult to assess what you are actually buying. To understand exactly what you'll pay and what you'll get for that payment, you need to do a thorough job of vetting the fund or advisor you're considering, ask for recommendations, and read through all of that fine (and boring) print in the prospectus. Or, you can avoid most fees altogether, and use the information we cover next to find and buy a solid index fund that will need little management and keeps fees to a minimum.

Finding Low-Fee Index Funds

It can be close to impossible to find a managed stock fund, such as those made up of A and B class shares, that will have strong enough returns to compensate for the fund's management fees, when compared to an index fund. Every time a fund manager buys or sells a stock or bond, the trade costs money. That cost is covered by the fund's management fee, the yearly fee charged for running the fund and, in some cases, to help pay for the services of the investment advisor or advisor team, along with other administrative costs. The management fee typically is included as part of the expense ratio. Nearly every fund charges a management fee but, as you probably have guessed, index funds tend to charge lower management fees because they require less management. Less buying and selling translates to fewer trading costs.

As we've seen, management fees can take a big divot out of the fund's returns. Bill McNabb, the CEO of Vanguard, noted in a recent publication that over the last 10 years 82% of managed stock funds and 81% of managed bond funds have failed to beat their index or have gone out of business.[57] In other words, if we invest in a managed fund, we have about one chance in five of actually doing better than the index, after we deduct the costs of fees from the profits our investment has earned. The chart shown in Figure 7.4 compares the costs and returns of a collection of *large cap* or large company funds. The Vanguard fund in the first column is an S&P 500 Index fund; the others are managed funds.

FIGURE 7.4: A COMPARISON OF COSTS AND RETURNS AMONG SOME LARGE CAP FUNDS. [58]

	Vanguard 500 Index Fund Investor shares	American Funds Fundamental Investors F	Dreyfus Appreciation Fund	Fidelity Large Cap Stock Fund	Oppenheimer Rising Dividends
Expense Ratio	0.14%	0.68%	0.94%	0.62%	1.08%
1-year	21.67%	23.27%	26.64%	18.15%	10.05%
3-year	11.26%	12.72%	9.80%	10.11%	4.54%
5-year	15.62%	15.43%	11.72%	15.41%	10.05%
10-year	8.37%	8.00%	6.89%	8.55%	5.54%

In fairness, some of the funds I've chosen for this chart have actually beaten the market index over short or long periods of time. For example, The Fidelity Large Cap Stock Fund did the best of all the funds over a 10-year period, but not in the 5-year and 1-year periods. The American Fund, on the other hand, was consistently good during the period of time reviewed for this comparison. If recent past performance is the main indicator, American wins but the long term, 10-year best performance goes to Fidelity although the Vanguard S and P 500 is just a shade behind. The Oppenheimer fund lagged behind the others. Which fund had the highest fees?

The data on this chart proves my point; past performance does not assure future performance because managers and companies change. That's what makes S&P 500 index funds, with their long history of average performance, so attractive to so many investors. Yes, you would have made slightly better returns over the long run had you chosen the Fidelity Large Cap Stock Fund rather than the Vanguard S&P 500 fund, but that choice would have involved a big dose of investment savvy and an even larger dose of luck (and risk) after all, there are more than 12,000 mutual funds and ETFs to choose from. The odds are that you—or I or any individual investor—would have chosen a fund that did *worse* than the S&P. For me, I choose to take the sure bet and get rich.

Victor's Advice

I don't keep all of my investment eggs in one basket, and you shouldn't feel compelled to do that, either. I have funds invested with multiple companies, including Vanguard, American Funds, Fidelity, and others. If you decide to handle your own investing, be sure to check the prospectus of any fund you're considering, so you can be sure that the fees they're charging seem fair and reasonable and check the fund's performance over time. Strong, long-term performance typically indicates a well-managed fund. Wherever you invest, though, I recommend that index funds should be the core of your investment strategy.

If you decide to invest in bond funds, you need to especially cautious about fees and expenses. Overall, bond fund fees represent a much higher percent of your investment results than do the fees charged by stock mutual funds. Some bond funds are index funds, so they don't require a lot of hands-on management. Others are actively managed, however, which can drive up the bond fund's management fees and overall expense ratios. The chart shown in Figure 7.5 compares four managed bond funds, their five-year returns, fees, and expense ratios.

FIGURE 7.5: A COMPARISON OF EXPENSES AND RETURNS FOR FOUR MANAGED BOND FUNDS.[59]

Average annual performance— quarter end 12/31/17	Vanguard Long-Term Treasury Adm.	Vanguard Long-Term Treasury Inv.	T. Rowe Price U. S. Treasury Long-Term Fund Investor	PIMCO Long-Term U.S. Government Fund Class A
Expense Ratio	0.10%	0.20%	0.51%	1.00%
1-year	8.69	8.58	8.22%	4.61%
3-year	2.76%	2.66%	2.26%	1.00%
5-year	3.45%	2.35%	2.78%	2.16%
10-year	6.47%	6.35%	6.15%	6.24%

As you can see in this comparison, the fund with the lowest expense ratio is also the one with the highest five- and ten-year returns. Higher fees make it very difficult to beat funds with lower fees for several reasons. First, the returns are lower on bonds and as a result, the fees represent a higher percentage of the return. Second, we can't count on funds that outperform their peers one year to continue to do that over the long term--in fact, analysis has revealed that they don't.[60]If you've reached this point in the chapter and have decided that getting a handle on fund fees is going to occupy way too much of your brain space, take heart. It may be that in the very near future advisors will have to forgo recommending expensive loaded funds for any pension plan investor.

A new class of funds called "T" shares has been introduced to meet the fiduciary rule for pension funds that, at the time of this writing, its adoption has been delayed by the Department of Labor until 2019. We talked about T shares and this rule earlier in the chapter, but in essence, the rule's based on a fiduciary standard established back in 1940's Investment Advisors Act, which states that advisors have to put their clients' interests above their own when it comes to making investment recommendations. What this means is that fees and expenses for investing should continue on their years-long downward trajectory. No matter how far these fees decline, however, some investors will always want and need advice. And, no matter what the regulatory situation may be at any given time, it's up to us, as investors, to take an active role in managing our money—even when that means overseeing the people doing that management for us. Whether you pay an hourly fee for investment advice or the regularly charged expense ratio and load fees charged by the funds themselves, it's up to you to determine that what fees you'll pay, whether those fees are reasonable, and how well they fit with your overall goals for getting rich from your investments.,

Victor's Advice

When you've found and chosen an investment or an investment advisor, your work isn't over. You still have to continually monitor the performance of either the fund or the advisor. Read your quarterly statements and watch your investments' performance over time. If at any point the returns or fees no longer meet your needs and expectations, get on the phone with your fund manager or investment advisor, get an explanation, and if necessary, move your investments to a more stable or lucrative option.

Getting the Goods from a Prospectus

Throughout this chapter we've overviewed the many, often obscure fees that investment advisors and mutual fund companies may charge shareholders. We've also seen how important it is to know what fees a fund *is* charging, and how much those fees add up to. Where do we find out about a fund's fees and expenses? Most investment companies provide some of this information online, where investors can find it as easily as they find the fund's price quote. But the full accounting of the costs we'll pay for investing in any mutual fund is included in the mutual fund's prospectus.

If you've ever had investments on your own or through a 401K, you've undoubtedly been confronted at some point with a fund prospectus. You'd remember it as that inches-thick booklet that arrived in a plain white wrapper in the mail. A prospectus may contain hundreds of pages of fine print, interrupted occasionally by unreadable charts. Just flipping through the pages can leave you feeling overwhelmed and underprepared to ever understand, let alone manage, your investments. Many early investors will carry the prospectus directly from their mailbox to the nearest trash can and toss it away, with deep gratitude that they don't have to crack the thing's spine. That's another mistake investors make--and it's a big one.

As you might have guessed, the fund companies don't necessarily enjoy preparing and mailing out a prospectus. The SEC has rules require certain types of companies to provide investors with a prospectus at specific times, such as when they buy a security. Basically, a prospectus includes summaries of the investment proposals for the fund, as well as the classes of shares it offers and the fees it charges. Most investment companies have a short- and long-form prospectus, because reading the longer version is so tedious and boring that it might be unreasonable to expect the average investor to bother with it. But the really revealing information in any prospectus may be found in the SAI or *Statement of Additional Information* that typically appears in the long version of a prospectus.

This section of the prospectus, as uninviting as it may appear to be, offers vital information about just how and when the fund uses money that, ultimately, comes from shareholder profits. For example, one large and respected investment fund has a 221-page document that includes detailed SAI information about their fixed income funds. After going through more than 100 pages of the prospectus (you're welcome), I found the following statement, which I have abbreviated and *emphasized* in parts:

" ...or the Distributor may provide additional cash payments out of its own resources to financial intermediaries that sell shares of a fund or provide other services... Such payments are separate from any sales charges, 12b-1 fees and/or shareholder services fees or other expenses paid by the fund to those intermediaries. .... Cash compensation also may be paid from [company name] or the Distributor's own resources to Service Agents for inclusion of a fund on a sales list... *From time to time, [company name] or the Distributor also may provide cash or noncash compensation to Service Agents in the form of: occasional gifts; occasional meals, tickets or other entertainment; support for due diligence trips; educational conference sponsorships; support for recognition programs; technology or infrastructure support; and other forms of cash or non-cash compensation permissible under broker-dealer regulations. In some cases, these payments or compensation may create an incentive for a Service Agent to recommend or sell shares of a fund to you.*

Yeah, an all-expense-paid trip to a Vegas resort for an "educational conference" may be an incentive to sell people investments--who knows? There's an equally slim possibility that your dog might enjoy eating that steak you have sizzling on the grill.

After digging through the 433-page behemoth SAI of another large investment company prospectus, here's another interesting bit of prospectus info that I uncovered:

"...In addition to the payments described above, the Distributor and/or [company name] may make payments in connection with or reimburse financial firms' sponsorship and/or attendance at conferences, seminars or informational meetings ("event support"), provide financial firms or their personnel with occasional tickets to events or other entertainment, meals and small gifts ("other non-cash compensation"), and make charitable contributions to valid charitable organizations at the request of financial firms ("charitable contributions") to the extent permitted by applicable law, rules and regulations.

In other words, the parent company may use their profits to influence people who are "recommending" mutual funds to you for investment.

Ironically, with these disclosures, both companies actually admit that they may be unduly influencing advisors/brokers to sell their products. You wouldn't know this unless you read the expanded version of the prospectus SAI, which few investors do, and which I rarely did in the past. All of this influence peddling is legal, but can't we assume that it will cost us investors' money in the long run? Doesn't it stand to reason that the company will have to charge higher management fees for their funds in order to pay these costs? I seriously doubt that the companies will use money from their own pockets and profits to cover these costs; like any for-profit venture, consumers pay the costs in the end. When it comes to investment companies, we're the consumers.

So, what do we do? Here's my step-by-step plan for finding a low-fee index fund:

1. Go online and look up the available information for large mutual fund companies such as Vanguard, T Rowe Price, and Fidelity (there are others, so look thoroughly), who limit their management activities and fees.
2. Read what you find online, then request a prospectus for any fund that interests you.
3. Read the SAI information in the prospectus, just to be sure that you know what the fund is charging.
4. If the charges amount, in total, to 0.75% or 75 basis points more of the total assets invested, look at other companies. I personally try to find funds charging 30 basis points or less.
5. Choose a fund that has a good history of high returns and charges few, reasonably priced fees.

Sound simple? That's because it is. In general, these companies charge the lowest fees on a vast array of investment products, so in most cases, investors in the companies can't go far wrong. You may choose to do business with Dreyfus, PIMCO, American Funds, or other companies that offer a variety of funds with varying loads and fees. For example, when I was doing my research for this book, Dreyfus was offering a bond index fund available to institutional investors (such as your workplace) with management fees of 0.41% and sound returns. You just have to do some homework to find the funds that match your goals—and your expectations.

Making the Most of an Influence-Driven World

I know that a lot of the information we've reviewed in this chapter can be discouraging. The financial industry is complex and many of its methods, charges, and fees can be opaque—maybe even intentionally so. But, let's not forget that the financial industry isn't the only group that we could accuse of buying influence. As a physician, I have been wined and dined by many a drug company, under the guise of being educated about the benefits of the company's new drug, which in many cases was no better than a less-expensive drug made by another company. Fortunately, regulations have improved over the years, and now many of the once-common forms of pharmaceutical company influence peddling are controlled or even prohibited. Even though I miss the $70.00 bottles of wine, I get it. Companies shouldn't be able to buy access to a doctor's prescription pad.

The same is true for the financial industry. Over the years, waves of regulation have come and gone that have shifted the way investment companies can 'encourage' brokers and advisors to push their products to investors for a fat commission or other perk, regardless of the investment's benefits for the hapless buyer. In the end, however, no amount of regulation will keep you from losing investment profits if you don't read between the lines. Investment companies must make profits, and they do so out of fees and expenses from our mutual fund investments. We investors are only in the game to build our own wealth, though, so it's up to us to make sure that we maximize the returns we can gain from investing our money. And the more money a company spends on marketing, promotion, and "influence," the more fees they'll have to charge, and the lower our returns will be.

In spite of this chapters required heavy lifting, I hope you've arrived at the end convinced that your time and mental energy was well spent. We have to invest if we want to get rich, so even a mutual fund with generous fees and loads is a better option than not saving and investing at all or trying to time the market by buying and selling individual stocks on our own. So, we have to do our homework, keep our eyes open—for as long as we hold and use our investments.

That last point is critical. Just because we've chosen an investment or an investment advisor, we can't just go to sleep and count on the returns to mount up. In fact, in every area of life, we can't turn over our brain *or* our wallet to any one person or company, no matter how much we trust them. We're adults and we have to maintain the ultimate responsibility for managing and building our wealth. That means checking our quarterly statements, gauging the progress of our investments over time, and making sure they're continuing to work for us. Remember, investing isn't like winning the lottery. It won't make us rich overnight. But if you invest regularly over the long haul and pay attention to where your money is being invested and how much your investments cost, you will continue to build wealth—and you'll get rich. That's a goal worth working toward.

CHAPTER 8: KNOWING WHEN TO SAY YES

It's 2014 and the bond market has had a 20-year increase in prices, driving interest rates to new lows. In fact, the return on a 10-year treasury bond stands at only 2%. You're only a few years away from retirement and common wisdom tells you that you should have a greater proportion of your investment portfolio in bonds. But, with bond returns so low, is that a wise choice?

Question: Should you increase the proportion of bonds in your retirement fund?

Answer; YES. You should balance the proportions of stocks and bonds in your portfolio based on your age, not on the current price of bonds. As you get nearer to retirement, you should raise the proportion of bonds in your portfolio. I recommend doing this rebalancing every six months to a year.

Most people think investing is difficult, but I can tell you that it isn't. Saying NO to shaky personal loans, risky business, and well-run scams is difficult. Investing is easy because the principles behind successful investment are relatively simple, and they've been working well for decades. If you learn and follow the principles and processes we've covered in this book consistently over the course of several years, they will make you rich. In this chapter, we're going to bring a tighter focus to those ideas, so you can use them to make decisions about how, when, and with what investments you want to begin your own investment process. But first, here are the fundamentals of investing that you'll want to use as a basis for the decisions you'll be considering as you read through this chapter:

1. As an investor, you'll be buying stocks and bonds (preferably, in funds). Stocks represent equity and bonds represent debt.
2. When you buy stock in a company, you own a piece of that company—that's your equity.
3. When you buy a bond, CD, or money market fund, you have loaned money to a government, corporation, bank, or other organization—that makes you a creditor.
4. All investments involve risk. Investment values ebb and flow over time.

As we saw in Chapter 7, the simplest and most assured way to earn money on your investments is to invest in a diversified collection of stock index or bond index funds, and to invest regularly, consistently, and for an extended period of time. In this chapter, we're going to walk through the basics of saying YES to that process, by getting started as an investor in stocks and bond mutual funds. After a brief overview of the risks and rewards of those funds, we'll examine how to choose the fund that's right for you, and the tax implications of index fund investment. But, because index funds aren't the *only* smart investment option, we'll also cover the basics of getting started as an investor in exchange traded funds, money market funds, and CDs. We'll take one final look at the main culprits that investors face when trying to beat the odds in the markets, to help you prepare to smack-down those profit-killing practices in your own investment process. Finally, we'll explore a short series of critical questions whose answers can help you build the framework for your investing approach and the portfolio that will move you toward your investment goals. You can use the information in this chapter to create your own roadmap for building wealth and starting along the path toward becoming rich.

As I've said before, I'm not using this book as a platform to offer advice on specific investments. The best investments for you and your wealth-building plan will depend on your own set of "specifics," including your age, your goals, and your tolerance for risk. Any investment that any of us makes has the capacity to lose or make money; it's risk that makes an investment an investment. But, here, I offer some guidelines and useful questions that might make it easier for you to find the right investments for your needs—in other words, the investments that will increase your probabilities of pulling in strong returns over long periods of time. That's how people all over the world get rich from investing, and that's how *you're* going to get rich, too.

Getting Started in the Stock Market

Did you know I'm a part owner of Apple, Inc.? Well, it's true. That's because I own stock in the company. When you buy a company's stock, you are buying a share or equity in the company. There are about 5.24 billion shares (or pieces) of Apple stock *outstanding* or in the market place, so every share I own represents slightly less than one five-billionth of the company's ownership. So, no, I don't own enough of Apple to influence when its next iPhone release will take place, but I'm still a part-owner, and as such, I have the right to vote at the shareholders' annual meeting.

That's basically what stocks are all about. Companies sell us a piece of their operation and use the money we give them in trade to maintain and grow their business. As their operations grow and their profits (ideally) improve, the pieces of the companies we shareholders own become more valuable, so our investment value grows. We've talked about stocks and stock funds throughout the book, but now let's review just a bit more information that can help prepare you to get started as a stock market investor.

Saying YES to the Risks and Rewards

Investing in stock and bond index funds has many advantages, but it isn't a guaranteed passport to riches. On the positive side, you stand to make money in the long run owning stocks because, under the right circumstances, their profits *can* grow right along with the economy.

Many well-known companies, such as Coca-Cola, Johnson & Johnson, and 3M, have a record of increasing their dividends yearly over long periods of time and are represented in both the S&P 500 index and the Dow Jones Industrial Average index. Stocks also are a hedge against inflation, as they are able to adjust their prices depending on economic conditions. Your odds of making good money by holding stocks over a decade or more are very good. For example, out of the last 91 years, the S&P 500 Index has had positive gains during 67 of those years, or almost 74% of that time.

Short-term stock investments, on the other hand, can be risky, and taking on risk is perhaps the least-positive aspect of investment. Those who owned stocks during the depression years of 1929 through 1933 experienced four consecutive down years in the stock market. Those who lost or sold everything during that time had few investible assets to help recover their money as the market regained strength. Investors who engaged in panic selling when the Great Recession hit in March of 2009 also suffered permanent damage from a major hit to the stock market. Many lost half or more of their retirement nest egg as a result. Investors who hung on, however, ended up making a *lot* of money in just a few short years, as stock prices recovered and then soared.

And, that uptick may not take long at all. After the terrorist attacks of September 11, 2001, the New York Stock Exchange (NYSE) closed down in anticipation of panic selling, and it stayed closed until September 17th—the longest time the NYSE had closed since the Depression.[61] When trading resumed, the market lost 7.1% in the first day alone, a one-day record loss. By the end of that week, the S&P had lost 11.6%. Investors sold off airline stocks, financial industry stocks, insurance stocks, you name it, convinced that they had to sell in order to stem their losses. And yet, within just one month, the S&P, Dow Jones, and the NASDAQ had returned to their pre-September 11 prices.[62] The stock market itself was actually higher than it had been before the attack.

So, through a horrific terrorist attack and the bursting of two major financial bubbles, the stock market today still manages to be profitable for investors who ride out the storms. In classic finance textbooks, the benefits investors can gain from riding through those risks is called a *risk premium*, and that premium generally bumps investor returns by 5 to 6% above the returns earned by risk-free investments in CDs or treasury bonds. That's why we need to think of investing in the stock and bond markets as a long-term process, not a get-rich-quick scheme.

Victor's Advice

If you get out of the stock market when prices are low, it will seem painfully costly to get back in when prices tick back up.

Saying YES to Growth, Value, or Income

While stocks represent an incredibly vast variety of businesses, organizations, and ventures, most domestic stocks fall into one of three categories: growth, value, and income. The differences in the categories are framed by when and how shareholders stand to profit from their investments. We buy stocks because we want to make a profit on our money, either by "buying low and selling high," or by holding stocks for a long time and periodically raking in profits from them. I have recommended throughout this book that you invest in stock and bond mutual funds and index funds, so you can spend your spare time in more enjoyable ways than researching individual stocks and bonds. You can buy funds, though, that specialize in specific categories of stocks. So, it's a good idea to know what the stock categories are, what they say about the companies they represent, and how they shape the way stocks function for investors. Anyone signed up for a 401(k) has already been through this lineup, so I'll make it quick.

Stocks that appear to be underpriced based on their profits and sales are called *value* stocks. Value stocks typically are issued by larger companies that have been around for a while, and so they tend to be considered less risky. That doesn't mean they *are* less risky, of course. But companies that have experienced management and established practices tend to be more stable and better at fixing issues that can temporarily ding their value.

Income stocks grant dividends to shareholders, which those shareholders then can use as income. Income stocks tend to be issued by utilities and REITs. Both value and income stocks grant dividends to shareholders. As I write this chapter in March of 2017, the dividend rate for Apple is 1.61%. So, for example, if a shareholder owned 400 shares of Apple, those shares would have a value of $56,000, and the shareholder would score a yearly dividend of over $900, paid in quarterly installments.

Not all companies regularly pay dividends to their shareholders. Instead, when those companies make profits, they plow the money back into the company to help it grow—which is why stock in such a company is called a *growth* stock. Growth stocks typically are issued by younger, smaller, companies often in cutting edge industries such as tech or telecommunications. Facebook is a prime example of a growth-stock company. Instead of distributing quarterly dividends to shareholders, Facebook has used its profits to continually expand its operation and buy up other companies, such as Instagram. Facebook's stock has soared, along with its growth. The initial price for Facebook when it first went on the market back in 2012 was about $38 a share. The company went through a rocky first three months or so, but just five years later, Facebook stock was sitting at $170 a share with 2.889 billion shares outstanding, making it the fourth most valuable company in the NASDQ index just behind Amazon, Microsoft, and Apple. Of course, lots of things can knock a business off the cutting edge—inexperienced management, over-extended resources, development failure, you name it. In *every* investment, the greater the potential for profit, the greater the potential risk.

Most stock portfolios balance the ratio of growth and income stocks and bonds to match the age, goals, and risk tolerance of the investor—a process known as *asset allocation*. If you're near retirement and need to rely on your stocks for regular income, your portfolio probably will include a more income than growth stocks. If you're younger and able to tolerate a bit more risk in the quest to quickly beef up your investment returns, you may include a larger chunk of growth stocks in the mix. Many mutual funds, including index funds, specialize in specific balances of stocks in these categories. To find funds of a specific category, do some online research, and check the financial publications such as *Forbes, Kiplinger, The Wall Street Journal,* and others.

However you earn profits from your stock investments, at some point you will have to pay the price of those gains. That brings us to the issue of taxes.

Saying YES to the Tax (Wo)man

To remain perfectly legal, I once again have to tell you that I'm not offering the following information as specific or authoritative tax advice. You'll need to get that from your own research or, better yet, from a good accountant. Taxes are very complicated and changeable, so a good accountant can give you the best advice on how to best determine your tax liabilities. But, here's some general information about how profits from stock investments are taxed.

When you make a pile of money in the stock market, you have a lot to be grateful for. You also may have a bit of a tax bill to settle up at some point. The "when" and "how much" of that tax depends on the type of investment that's earned the profits. If your stocks or stock funds are held in a pension account, you probably won't have to pay any tax on the proceeds of those investments until you start to make withdrawals. If you hold the stock or index fund in your personal account for at least 60 days, and you receive dividends from it, you probably will need to pay a tax of 15% or 20% on those dividends, depending on your income tax bracket.

Some people live on dividends from stocks and mutual funds, and that's not a bad way to live at all. Taxes are higher on investments held a short period of time because the government doesn't view short-term trading as adding much to the overall economy, so they tax its profits as ordinary income. Which means that a buy-and-hold strategy not only increases your chances of making money in the long run, it has tax advantages as well. If you must take profits for the sale of a growth stock or mutual fund and you have held the security for a year, you pay what is called a *capital gains* tax which may be nothing for joint tax payers with less than $75,200 in income (if you hold the stock for less than a year, your earnings are considered short-term capital gains, and are taxed just like your regular income). For those earning more than that income just mentioned, the capital gains tax may be 15% or 20%, which is much less than if it the profits were taxed at regular income— that rate could be as much as 40% for the highest tax brackets. Again, you'll need to consult with a tax advisor to determine your tax bracket and necessary payments.

Victor's Advice

Remember, taxes in taxable accounts matter as much as fees when it comes to maximizing returns.

Saying YES to Investing (Wisely) in Bonds

Now, for a very brief primer on investing in bonds. As we've seen, when you own a bond or bond fund you have made a loan to a company (*corporate* bonds) or a government (*municipal* and *Treasury* bonds). That loan has to be paid back at a defined interest rate over the *duration* or life of the bond. Bonds durations can be as short as one year to as long as 30 years, and throughout the duration the agency that issued the bond pays investors regular interest payments, usually twice a year. At the end of the bond's duration the bond matures, and you get your principle or invested money back. The longer the bond's duration, the higher interest rate it generally pays to us investors because our money is tied up longer.

For simplicities sake, we can divide bonds into two categories, those that are taxable and those that aren't. Municipal bonds are non-taxable, which makes them appealing to some high-income investors. They also generally offer a lower interest rate, which helps the entity that issues them. Municipal bonds might be issued, for example, by a city in need of a new school or updated sewer system, and the city can raise money by issuing bonds, and keep the interest rate low on the money they're borrowing. Municipal bonds aren't taxable by the federal government but may trigger state and/or local taxes. Corporate bonds are taxed as regular income.

Bonds generally are considered a less risky investment than stocks because investors are really creditors who have loaned money out to a company or a government; that's different than buying a piece of a company in the hope that you can share in its future growth or profits. In the unlikely case of a bond-issuer's bankruptcy, bond holders get paid first before any stock holders. And, if the company hits hard times, it can reduce or even eliminate dividend payments to stock holders. Not so with bonds; even in hard times, as long as it isn't in bankruptcy the company is legally required to pay interest to bond holders. Of course, investors pay for this added layer of safety; bonds traditionally pay lower returns than those paid by the stock market. And, when we buy corporate bonds, we don't own a piece of the company the way we do when we buy stock, so we don't benefit from the company's future profits.

There's one risk with bonds that you don't suffer with stocks, however, and that's because bond values can shift with interest rates. If interest rates go up, the price—and therefore the value—of bonds goes down. So, if you are holding bonds during an interest rate spike, the value of the bonds you're holding will adjust down until the rate of return on your bond levels out to match the current interest rate. So, for example, let's say you invested $50,000 in a corporate bond fund when interest rates were at 4%. That fund would yield $2000 annually in interest (4% of $50,000). But if the interest rate increases to 4.25%, the value of your fund would go down to $47,059, giving you the same yield from interest that you would have received when the value was $50,000. That shift guarantees that new buyers of the bond can't buy in at a lower cost and get a higher yield.

The converse is true as well, the value of your fund goes up as interest rates go down. If interest rates fell to 3.75%, our example bond would have to be worth $53,333 to generate $2000 in income, so your bond fund would theoretically increase in value to keep your yield steady. The longer a bond's duration, the more sensitive it becomes to shifts in interest rates. You also have to be aware of the credit risks involved in bonds. If the company or government that issued the bond experiences economic struggles that make it questionable whether the issuer will be able to meet its interest requirements, the price of its bonds may go down. So, as an investor, you have to be aware of two risks in buying bonds—interest rate rises and increased credit risks--both can lower the price of the bonds in your portfolio.

Many investors use bonds to balance out the riskier investments in their portfolio, but they may not always succeed at doing that. In the 2008-2009 financial meltdown, for example, corporate bond values decreased moderately at times, but the value of government bonds actually increased. And, we need to remember that bonds held their value better than many stocks did during that time, so bond investments were still a reasonable hedge against a declining stock market, especially for conservative and older investors.

Victor's Advice

Economic issues can lower the price of bonds if there is concern that the issuing corporation(s) will have difficulty meeting debt obligations, which can happen during a recession. Even for governments, adverse political and economic conditions can cause a downgrade in credit for bond originators. That's what happened with U.S. Treasury bonds back in the summer of 2011, when congress was deadlocked on raising the debt ceiling. Bond prices drifted lower over uncertainty about how the US government would be paying its debts. Nevertheless, bond prices rebounded after the crisis resolution.

Saying YES to an Index Fund

John Bogle from the Vanguard Group launched the first index mutual fund in 1975, a fund grounded in the notion that the transaction fees involved in buying and selling stocks would, in the long run, consistently produce lower returns than investors could earn simply by buying a large group of stocks and going with whatever course the market takes-- up, down or sideways. Depending on your sources and how you calculate, the S&P 500 Index has averaged as high as 10.58% a year in growth for the past four decades. A $10,000 investment in a non-taxable mutual fund left to ride the market for those 40 years would be worth almost $669,000 today, and the investor would have had to do *nothing* with the account over all that time, other than open monthly statements and marvel at the growth of his or her investment. No buying, selling, thinking or worrying.

Back to the Basics

Way back in Chapter 1, I outlined the mutual fund basics. We've covered a lot of territory since then, so here's a quick recap: An index mutual fund buys stocks or bonds based on the value of the company or bond issuer, as reflected in its position within an index. When you redeem shares, the stocks or bonds will be sold in the same proportions. The top 10 companies in the S&P 500 index represent more than 50% of the index's value, and the top 30 companies out of the 500 represent more than 75% of the index. That means that 75% of every dollar you put into an S&P 500 index fund goes to buy stock in 30 companies.

Index mutual funds require very little in the way of management—or management fees. No active decision or costly research goes into whether to buy or sell an individual stock or bond. In essence, the market place decides which companies or bonds are more valuable, by bidding the price and value of the company shares or issuer's bonds up or down. The fund isn't trying to beat the marketplace, it's just mirroring it. And that's the beauty of the index. When a stock or bond becomes more valuable, it moves up in the index roster and the mutual fund ups its investments in that stock or bond; when a stock or bond sinks in value, it also sinks in the fund along with the fund's investments in that particular stock or bond. Meanwhile, we investors do nothing, and we pay very low transaction and management fees, while benefiting from the mutual fund's ongoing portfolio tweaking. These funds are incredibly inexpensive to run. Fidelity's institutional Standard and Poor's 500 Index, which often is available through a company IRA, has (as I write this chapter) an expense ratio of just 0.03% % or 3 basis points.[63]

A bond index has the same risks as individual bonds. The value of the index will increase or decrease as interest rates go down and up and the longer the maturity of the bond fund the more volatile its returns may be. However, the longer the bond index goes out the higher the return on the interest rates. Because there are so many bonds the risk to the index of any individual bond default is low. Bonds can be a bit more difficult to track in an index, simply because there are so many issuers that the mutual fund index may not be able to track them all. But outliers make up a very small percentage of the total bond market, so this is a relatively minor issue. The most widely used bond index is the Bloomberg Barclays Aggregate Bond Index from which the Vanguard Total Bond Index and Fidelity US bond index fund are modeled. As of February 2017, 62.1% of the Vanguard Index was in US government issues.

Why Would I Say NO?
So why doesn't everyone simply invest in an index fund? That's a reasonable question. I think the answer goes back to the questions we

batted around in Chapter 2: Are you above average in just about everything? Today, everyone's the star of their own movie, so all of us are above average, right? And, if we're above average in choosing investments and timing the market, can't we count on scoring returns that will make that index look paltry?

That *could* happen. After all, there are a handful of investors out there who, in all of the market's history, have consistently beaten the index. So, any investor who thinks they can match the results of Peter Lynch at the Fidelity Magellan Fund in the 80s, John Neff from Wellington Management who ran one of the best performing funds in history, the Vanguard Windsor Fund, for more than thirty years, or Larry Puglia from T. Rowe Price Blue Chip Growth, should go for it. Two of the three folks I just named are retired now, so the market place is looking for new "giants" to take their place. But, I'll never count on my own ability to match these exceptionally savvy investors at beating the market—not over a long period of time, certainly. There are over 9000 mutual funds to sort through, and I don't trust myself to successfully mine the rare gems hidden among them. The Blue-Chip Growth fund may be a very good investment right now, for example, but there's is no guarantee that it's going to continue to beat the market in the future. In fact, a number of studies have shown that one year's hot mutual funds often are laggards in subsequent years.

In other words, it's easier to explain why I invest in index mutual funds, than it is to speculate as to why others don't. But as you make your investment decisions, bear in mind how much you feel willing—and able—to do the work necessary to beat the market. No matter what your level of confidence might be in your ability to beat the market, I strongly advise you to avoid trying. It's too easy to get sucked into buying last year's darling of a stock, only to find out that it's turned into this year's dog. Trying to time the market is a sucker's game—one I advise you to avoid.

If you want to avoid spending the majority of your time sniffing around, reading, and thinking about investing, you can simply invest in an index fund. Then, you can use all of your extra time doing something less painful than investment research and trading—such as working out on your elliptical. And here's the best news—you'll do better in your returns than any of the folks around you who are trying to take their place among the world's tiny number of stock savants.

Saying YES to the ETF

The ETF or *exchange traded fund* is a remarkable and relatively new entry into the investment universe. These are mutual funds, including indices, which trade like stocks. You can buy and sell shares in an ETF, with the value based on the net asset value of the fund's underlying securities, including stocks, bonds, or commodities. While mutual funds are priced and traded at the end of a trading day, ETFs are traded throughout the day. That's a fact, not a huge advantage for the long-term investor. Two main advantages ETFs *do* offer, however, are their relatively low expense ratios and tax advantages; share owners don't have to declare capital gains taxes until they sell shares (bond ETF interest is usually generated monthly and taxed at the bond holder's marginal tax rate). Mutual funds, on the other hand, declare capital gains on profits from stock sales yearly, for which share owners must pay annual taxes.

There are thousands of ETFs out there covering almost every conceivable index and mutual fund orientation. Blackrock (IShares), Vanguard, and State Street are three reputable companies that have developed ETFs. I've invested in ETFs for years. A decade ago, I bought an ETF with SPY, a company that tracks the S&P 500 and has an expense ratio of .09% or 9 basis points. The investment was in a charitable foundation account I hold at Fidelity, and the expenses were lower than any index fund I thought I could get from Fidelity at the time. I recently sold an S&P index fund and a bond index fund at T. Rowe Price and used the proceeds to buy an Iboxx investment-grade corporate bond and more SPY, because their expense ratios were lower than I could get from an equivalent mutual fund index at T. Rowe Price. While I have accounts at Fidelity, T. Rowe Price, and Vanguard--all great companies with excellent products and services for the investor--I still can shop around for the best deal. ETFs allow me to do that quite easily.

Safe and Simple: Money Market Fund and CDs

Some people love the classics, and when it comes to investment, money market funds and CDs are about as classic as it gets. A *money market fund* is basically very short-term loan an investor makes to the institution managing the fund, and it's an investment option that carries a low interest rate and very low risk. While, unlike bank deposits, money market funds aren't insured by the FDIC, they generally are considered fairly safe and offer a somewhat higher interest rate than most checking or savings accounts. Money market funds come in a variety of forms, including tax free funds and funds that invest in US government securities. Many investment companies offer check-writing privileges on these accounts.

A CD or *certificate of deposit* is very much like a bond except it is issued by a bank, and it has a defined interest rate, holding period, and penalty for early withdrawal. Similar to a passbook savings account, CDs are insured by the FDIC (Federal Deposit Insurance Corporation) for up to $250,000. CDs pay a relatively lower interest rate than a corporate bond, however, because of their safety. CDs, money markets, even passbook savings accounts all serve essentially the same purpose for the issuer. You loan the bank or investment firm money, they pay you a low interest rate, then use the money you've loaned them to give mortgages to home buyers at a much higher interest rate than you're receiving. That's how banks and financial institutions make a profit.

Victor's Advice

If you have a chunk of money that you don't want to tie up in a long-term investment, rather than letting it lie dormant in a traditional checking or savings account, you can put that money in a money market fund. When you do, you're investing in short term, highly rated debt that will mature in less than a year. While almost all of them offer a relatively low interest rate, money market funds keep a stable net asset value—meaning the value doesn't fluctuate like that of a stock or bond--and some investors, like myself, use them instead of a bank account.

Beating the Odds when Saying YES

With all of these great investments around how does the average investor do? Well, according to DALBAR, Pretty badly. DALBAR is a company that tracks how investor behavior influences results, and how those results compare to the stock and bond indices on a yearly basis. DALBAR's 22nd annual Quantitative Analysis of Investor Behavior for the period ending 12/31/2015 includes a comparison between how the S&P 500 index and the Barclays Aggregate Bond Index performed over periods of one, five, 10, 20, and 30 years ending in 2015, and how the average investor in stocks and bonds performed during those same periods.[64] Figure 8.1 shows a chart, based on one included in the *DALBAR analysis, that illustrates that comparison.*

Figure 8.1A: A comparison of results earned by the S&P 500 Index, Barclay's Aggregate Bond Index, and average investors.

Stock (Equity) Returns
Average Investor

Number of years	S and P 500 Index	Average Investor	Difference
30	10.35	3.66	-6.69
20	8.19	4.67	-3.52
10	7.31	4.23	-3.08
5	12.57	6.92	-5.65
1	1.38	-2.28	-3.66

Figure 8.1B: A comparison of results earned by the S&P 500 Index, Barclay's Aggregate Bond Index, and average investors.

Bond (Fixed Income) Returns

Number of years	Barclays Aggregate Bond Index	Average Investor	Difference
30	6.73	0.59	-6.14
20	5.34	0.51	-4.83
10	4.51	0.39	-4.12
5	3.25	0.1	-3.15
1	0.55	-3.11	-3.66

Source: "Quantitative Analysis of Investor Behavior, 2016," DALBAR, Inc. www.dalbar.com

While the Standard and Poor's 500 Index returned an average 10.35% yearly for the thirty-year period ending 2015 the average investor only made 3.66%--that's a whopping 6.69% difference. Twenty-, 10-, 5- and one-year returns were lousy as well. Bond return differences were even worse relative to return. The average bond investor actually made nothing or was hit with a negative return when we consider the average inflation rate of 3%.

Based on the DALBAR data, here are some of issues that eroded the average investment returns included in the study:

- **Delayed Investment**: Delaying investment due to a lack of available cash represented a total of 15% of the investor shortfall.

- **Unplanned need for cash for other purposes**: DALBAR describes this issue as "the percentage of investor return that is lost or gained by withdrawing the investment before the end of the period being measured."[65] This issue contributed 19% of the total shortfall between the investor returns and the index returns.

- **Fees and expenses**: Fees and expenses made up 23% of the shortfall in investor returns. Of course, fees take a more substantial bite out of the returns of investors who dart in and out of the market than those of investors who follow a buy-and-hold strategy in broad stock and bond indices

- **Investor behavior**: The major cause of the shortfall, some 43%, was due to investor behavior. According to DALBAR'S analysis, this behavior included trying to time the market, which resulted in leaving the market too late after a plunge and entering too late as the market rebounded. Another pernicious problem for the average investor was the short holding times for investments.

The pie chart in Figure 8.2 is based on the DALBAR data and graphically illustrates these contributors to the individual investors' shortfall in comparison to index funds' performance.

FIGURE 8.2: INDIVIDUAL INVESTOR SHORTFALL CONTRIBUTORS

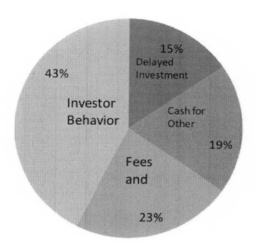

What investor behaviors interfered with their returns? Part of the answer to that question lies in the behavioral investing "tics" we covered in Chapter 2. Most investors are psychologically risk averse, so they tend to stay on the sidelines during the start of a bull market, when they could buy in and watch their investments climb. Secondly, loss and regret aversion keep people out of the market after a decline, when prices are low and "bargains" are easier to come by. Then there's the psychological inertia and status quo bias that encourage investors to keep their money safely where it is and wait until the herd pushes them to invest. At that point, prices have already gone back up and investing becomes more expensive. In essence, when average investors try to time the market, they consistently lose. Finally, many investors also fail to hold stocks long enough to fully reap their rewards. DALBAR reports that it's uncommon for the investors examined in their report to hold stock or bond mutual funds for more than four years. In comparison, asset allocation investors (people who own stocks and bonds and move the money back and forth between stock and bonds without selling all of any one investment class) held their funds slightly longer--for 4.6 years, on average.

A market cycle from boom to bust may be from four to 30 years. The most recent bull market has, as of this writing, lasted for eight years, making it one of the longest in history. The average investor is not likely to take full advantages of bear market by snapping up bargains. Even fewer investors are able to consistently jump out of the market in time to avoid all disasters. In fact, based on the DALBAR data, it appears to me that the average investor has specialized in buying high and selling low. I can assure you that I, a physician with an MBA and a long history and great interest in following the markets, wasn't able to predict the length and severity of the Great Recession, so how could we expect the average working man or woman with little to *no* interest in the markets to have done so? Whatever the reasons for the discrepancy in results, DALBAR's report reinforces the idea that most investors would be financially better off riding an index fund rather than trying to buy and sell individual stocks or funds through frequent trading.

Victor's Advice

I think I should note here that not everyone agrees with the methodology or even the conclusions DALBAR seems to imply with these findings. In essence, there's a broad school of thought that contends that investment advisors may earn the money they charge in fees by, perhaps, helping hapless investors avoid falling victim to their own investment misbehaviors.[66] That perspective may hold some value. Here's my opinion: If an advisor can keep you from doing stupid things with your investments, they may well be worth a modest fee. *But you always need to make sure those fees are low.* You should *never* count on high fees and expenses to pay off in better returns.

Are You Ready to Say YES? A Short, Self-Guided Q&A

Okay, so I've already said that I believe it's tougher to say NO to bad investments than it is to say YES to sound investments. If you want to master the tough stuff of investing, therefore, you have to determine whether you're ready to say YES, and just what you're ready to say YES *to*. To determine just what type of investment fund, model, or vehicle you should sock your money into, you need to answer four questions. Let's take a look at each of them, individually.

1. Am I investing or saving?

The answer depends on how soon you think you'll need to lay hands on the money in your investment, a period known as your *time horizon*. If you think you'll need it within one to five years, you basically have what's called a *savings time horizon*. In that case, you may be better off stashing your cash in money market funds or short-term bonds with little price fluctuation.

An *investing time horizon,* on the other hand, typically extends from five to thirty years. The longer your investing time horizon extends, the more diversification you may want to include in the combination of stocks, bonds, and money market funds within your investment portfolio. If you can leave the money alone for a longer period of time, you may want to put some of your money in stocks or stock funds, for example, with an increasing percentage allocated to that category over time. Price fluctuations will be greater over these longer periods, but so will your returns.

2. What is my tolerance for risk?

Nobody likes to lose, but a fear of losing takes more of a toll on some of us than it does on others. And the stock market, with its daily gyrations of one or two percentage points (and sometimes more), gives us a never-ending reason to be on guard against instability in the value of our investments. Your ability to ride the waves of increasing and decreasing values without being engulfed by anxiety plays a role in determining where you're better off investing your money. Risk tolerance is one of the critical factors in determining how you allocate your investments in higher-risk stocks and stock funds, lower-risk bonds and bond funds, and lowest risk money markets, CDs and savings accounts.

Determining just how comfortable you are with risk may take more than a simple moment of soul-searching. But never fear, there's an app for that. Actually, there are multiple risk tolerance questionnaires available online to help you step through the process of putting your risk tolerance on the table, including those from Morningstar investment research firm, Vanguard investments, and even the Rutgers University New Jersey Agricultural Experiment Station![67] Of course, there's also some controversy surrounding the ability of these quizzes to accurately assess risk tolerance because, as financial planning strategist and blogger Michael Kitces, has noted, "...neither regulators, academics, nor advisors themselves, even have agreement on exactly what key factors of a client's "risk profile" should be evaluated in the first place."[68] In other words, these quizzes give us stronger insights for making our decisions, but they can't make those decisions for us.

Still, your time may be well spent working through a few risk tolerance quizzes, to help you at least explore how you define risk, how you perceive risk, and how capable you are of maintaining *your* stability when the markets have temporarily lost theirs. In addition to gauging your personal comfort-level with risk, these assessments also may factor in your age, income, and other factors (more about these factors in the next section of this chapter). Some risk tolerance quizzes stick with basic questions such as "How long do you intend to hold onto this investment" and "What goals do you have for your investments." Others ask questions aimed below the surface, to uncover concepts of risk, loss, and recovery that you may not even realize you hold. Let's consider your answer to this question, one that you're likely to encounter in multiple questionnaires:

You buy a stock index fund and it goes down in price over the next month by 5%. Would you

    A. Buy more
    B. Sell, and put your money in a money market fund

If you have no risk tolerance at all, you probably chose B—get out of the market and stop losing money! But, if you are more risk tolerant (and you've read the previous chapters of this book), you probably answered A—buy more of the fund. You'll get a bargain while the prices are down and then you can just wait for the market to tick back up and pull your returns up with it. Of course, the market also could go lower; that's the risk you take. Will you have the guts to buy when others are afraid to open their wallets?

While many of these quizzes were created to help financial advisors determine what a clients' risk tolerance has to say about how much of their nest egg should be in stocks, bonds or money market funds, you can use the results of these quizzes to help make the same determinations about your own investment choices.

3. Do I want to build my own investment portfolio, or let an asset allocation fund determine the best mix?

Your level of risk tolerance isn't the only factor to consider when building a portfolio of individual stock and bond mutual funds, index funds, and ETFs. Your income, marital and family status, age, gender, and other factors also play a role in determining what mix of investment types you should include in your portfolio. Many brokerage firms and investment companies use an asset allocation model to create asset allocation funds that periodically change their mix of stocks, bonds and money market funds, depending on the investor's time horizon, risk tolerance, and other demographic factors. Most asset allocation funds invest in both American and foreign stocks and bonds to offer better diversification.

Victor's Advice

Foreign investments are a feature of asset allocation funds, not a bug. Many inexperienced investors tend to favor their own nation's investment options, and completely overlook big international opportunities for strong investment returns. China, for example, has been an economic powerhouse for some time and that means it should merit some exposure in long-term investment accounts. Asset allocation does this all for you in group of funds. I really like this approach if you can find funds that charge low fees. An asset allocation fund may be your best choice, which often includes domestic and international stocks along with bonds.

If you are saving to buy a house, for example, your investment choices are easy. You need to opt for the most conservative and safe investments, because any loss could stall your efforts to save for a down payment. Since you'll probably want the money in three years or less, money market funds or short-term CDs short term bond funds would be a good idea. If you have a slightly longer investment time horizon, the big investment companies can make your choices even easier with an asset allocation fund. As I write this chapter, Vanguard, for example, lists an asset allocation fund on its web site (vanguard.com) called the Life Strategy Income Fund (VASIX) for investors with a three-to-five-year time horizon. That fund invests 20% in stocks and 80% in bonds of intermediate maturity; it has a 5-year return rate of 4.12% and fees of 0.12% (12 basis points). Vanguard also offers longer-term recommendations for your personal investments, such as its Life Strategy Growth Fund. Investors with moderate risk tolerance and an investment time horizon longer than five years can take advantage of that fund, which has had a 7.98% yearly return since its inception in

1994.The fund invests 80% of its assets in stocks and 20% in bonds, and it charges fees of 15 basis points a year. Other asset allocation funds are available from a number of companies, each targeted toward specific investor demographics and risk tolerance.

I'm all for making your own investment decisions whenever possible, so you can save money on fees and expenses. At the same time, asset allocation funds and models can give new investors a firm platform on which to launch their investment practices. Determining the right asset allocation for your portfolio is one of the most important decisions you'll make as an investor. It doesn't hurt to get some help with that process, at any stage in your investment timeline. As I mentioned earlier, you need to find a fund that charges low fees (remember, you want your total fees and expenses to be 75 basis points or 0.75% or less), and then assess the fund carefully to make sure that its asset mix makes sense for your age, goals, income, risk tolerance, and so on. Forget about finding the perfect fund; as we've seen, the market is too changeable to offer any guarantees for any investment portfolio. Instead, focus on choosing a fund that you can live with—no emotional rollercoaster, no sleepless nights, no stress-induced panics.

Victor's Advice

Now, you can get advice from *roboadvisors,* companies that charge low fees and use computer algorithms and ETFs to make investment and asset allocation recommendations. *Betterment* (www.betterment.com) and *Wealthfront* (www.wealthfront.com) are two players in this arena. Roboadvisors charge low fees of 25 to 40 basis points and typically have low minimum account level requirements.

4. Do I want my money to go into a taxable personal account or a non-taxable retirement account?

If you're in one of the highest tax brackets, congratulations! As an investor, though, you'll need to be aware of the issue of taxation in your personal accounts. To build real wealth, your portfolio will need to include both retirement funds, which are non-taxable until withdrawal at the time of your retirement, and personal funds, which are taxed as you go. When you hold taxable accounts, however, you have to remember that you will be taxed on earned interest at your marginal tax rate and on dividends and capital gains at a rate that may be much lower than your marginal tax rate. Because you don't trade index funds frequently, they don't generate much capital gains and are held in a taxable account.

For high-tax-bracket investors, tax-free municipal bonds can be very attractive, because their interest is exempt from federal income tax. If the bonds come from in-state issuers, investors also may be able to avoid paying any state and local taxes on the bonds' interest. [69] Aside from the interest rate risk, tax-free municipal bonds can be good mutual fund investments in general for investors in higher tax brackets. Buying and selling individual bonds can be difficult due to the number of issuers and small markets for sales. A mutual fund, on the other hand, will buy large numbers of bonds and get discounts on the trading fees—and it enables you to buy and sell small amounts of the fund.

Making these decisions about taxable versus non-taxable accounts can be a tricky business. I can have a hard time deciding how much of my personal investments to put into stocks versus bonds, for example, so I was happy to find the Vanguard tax-managed balanced fund (VTMFX), which has almost 48% stock and 52% in intermediate tax-free bonds. The fund is managed with taxes in mind, so it generates mostly tax-free bond interest and capital gains, which are taxed at 15%--a much lower rate than general income tax, which can rise as high as nearly 40% for those in higher income brackets.

By the time this book goes to print, you may be able to find a fund that meets or beats these numbers; do a little research and see what you can turn up. In general, though, be aware that during the majority of your years as an investor, taxable accounts will form an important part of your portfolio, so you'll need to do what you can to keep taxes you'll owe as low as possible. Perhaps the simplest way to minimize taxes in these accounts is to invest in index funds, dividend paying stock funds, and tax free municipal bond funds. That way, you can have the benefits of those taxable investments, while lessening the sting of taxes.

And Now for the Big Question...

We all have a different definition of "success," and that means there's no one definition of what it takes to succeed as an investor. It also means we have to fully understand more than just our goals and skills as investors. To hit our *own* definition of successful investing, we have to have a very solid understanding of our expectations. Yes, our investment returns will be shaped by our decisions. But investing is a process we learn over time, and a skill we develop as our knowledge and experience of investing grow along with our judgment. To begin that journey on solid ground, we need a very clear vision of what we hope to achieve, as well as what we can expect to experience along the way. Only we can know whether or not we've prepared ourselves for the realities of the risks and opportunities that lie ahead. That preparation is the most effective tool we have for becoming successful investors.

That's not to say we have to go it alone. Remember that, in spite of my overall advice to avoid as many fees and expenses as possible in order to maximize your returns, I'm not trying to discourage you from finding and working with a good financial advisor. In fact, I think it's a good idea, as long as you do some homework, so you can be sure you aren't paying too much in fees, loads and expenses. But whether you're making your own investments or partnering with an investment pro, you still have to take responsibility for achieving your goals. No one will understand what *your* success looks like as much as you do, and no one else will care as much about whether you achieve that success, either.

And, no matter how successful we are as investors, we'll never be able to predict, let alone control, market results. Whether a stock or bond goes up in value on any day is, in the end, equivalent to a flip of a coin; there's a 50% chance of prices increasing and 50% chance of prices decreasing. Looking long term, the stock market as a whole is up two-thirds of the time and down one out of three days, but conditions can change dramatically in a very short time due to very unpredictable factors, including investor behavior. That volatility and unpredictably makes short-term investing and trying to time the market bad strategies in general. But dramatic losses can lead at dramatic gains for those willing to take the risk and stay in for the long haul, as markets have a chance to repair after damaging developments. Are you ready for that kind of ride? And are you clear about where you want your investment decisions to take you? If the answer to those questions is YES, you're well on your way to making the kinds of investment decisions that will build your future wealth.

YES or NO? Making the Decisions that Will Make You Rich

Does it feel like you're closer to understanding why, when, how, and in what you want to invest your money? I know that I started off this chapter by saying investing is easy, but I also know that making *any* decision that involves money can feel like a very difficult process. And investment decisions are particularly weighty, because they affect how you spend your money today, and how long your money will last throughout all of your tomorrows. At the same time, you've now been through a crash course in investment that should have prepared you to tackle these decisions from a strong platform of confidence *and* informed understanding. And, above all, you've had a whole book's worth of coaching on the absolute necessity of learning to say NO if you want to become rich.

Believe me, I don't expect this book to be your sole source of information and support as you make these critical investment decisions. Throughout the book, I've tried to add plenty of notes and links to other resources, including investment advisors, investment companies, financial analysis, research findings, professional opinions, and more. The more investment decisions you decide to take on yourself, the more time I advise you to spend doing your own research. Talk to experienced friends, family, and advisors, read personal finance and investing publications, both in print and online, and find the answers to the questions you develop along the way.

Any reputable financial advisor or broker should be willing to meet with you without a commitment to invest, and most of the large companies will discuss some recommendations over the phone. Fidelity offers Investors Solutions, for example, which can offer guidance on risk tolerance, asset allocation, and other basic investing issues. T. Rowe Price also offers a similar service to small investors, through "investment specialists" in its Client Development Department. Vanguard offers similar types of advice, as do most large, respected investment firms. Don't expect any of these sources to give you specific advice as to what fund or index to buy, but all of them should offer appropriate investment ideas for your individual needs.

In the end, we have to choose how we feel most comfortable saving and investing. The most important things to keep in mind as you make these choices, is the level risk you are taking on and your comfort with that risk. I've stated more than once in this book that all investments involve risks, but I've also shown you that some investments are much riskier than others, with outcomes that may be beyond anyone's capacity to predict. While stock and bond markets have known levels of risk, investing in businesses and loans to family and friends is something of a wild card; the only thing we know for sure about those investments is that the risk of losing everything is extremely high.

You can always opt to keep things simple, by stashing short-term savings in money market funds and CDs, and longer-term investments in stock and bond index funds with an asset allocation that's consistent with your tolerance for risk. In all of your investments, though, remember to keep fees low and forget about market timing. I hope that the information I've offered in this book has convinced you that you really can get started as an investor with a plan that's no more complex than that one. And, that saying NO—to behavioral investing, scams and schemers, risky business and personal loans, and exorbitant fees--is the most important skill you can develop in your long-term plan for building wealth.

Of course, putting that plan to work as we build a solid, healthy investment portfolio over the years ahead requires that we investors overcome two major hurdles: high emotions and high fees, in that order. We're going to have bad years, panics, and large short-term losses because of computer trading, political turmoil, and an ever-evolving universe of other political/social/environmental/economic disasters that can cause investors sleepless nights and anxious days. We're going to have difficulty saying NO to people and opportunities that we *want* to believe are good investments, but that we know are not. We're also going to be faced with the hair-raising experience of investing during a bear market, which requires that we have the guts to say YES when the rest of the investment-buying herd is screaming NO. But, I encourage you to use the information we've covered here, along with the best advice, guidance, and insights you can gather from your other, ongoing research to help stem your investment anxieties and sleep easily. Remember, we live in the United States, a country with free markets and a strong, long-lived democracy. Like the markets themselves, no matter what ill winds and economic storms may come, we investors will weather them. We can be held down only so long before we bounce back, and sometimes we're actually made stronger by the disasters we survive. But we need to be in the game to take advantage of the country's success, and the best way to step up to play is to begin investing wisely in our own future--today.

GLOSSARY OF INVESTMENT TERMS

12b-1 fee: A Security and Exchange Commission rule that allows mutual funds to compensate advisors, record keepers, and brokers for services related to fund transaction and maintenance, in addition to paying for advertising and promotion.

Actively managed mutual fund: A mutual fund in which a manager or group of advisors actively buy and sell stocks and bonds in an attempt to do better than the general market. Actively managed accounts fail to beat their comparative index more than 75% of the time.

Asset allocation: The division of funds among various investment options within an investment portfolio. *Asset allocation funds* periodically change their mix of stocks, bonds and money market funds, depending on the investor's time horizon, risk tolerance, and other demographic factors.

Basis Point: One hundredth of a percent, or 0.01%. Investment professionals use the term to describe differences in yields, interest rates, and so on. A 1.5% fee for managing your stock mutual fund is 150 basis points. This is one of the most important words to know, especially when you are talking to investment advisors.

Behavioral investing: A term used to describe investment decisions influenced by our psychological tendencies, preconceptions, and aversions rather than hard data. Investor behavior is a powerful force that can influence the marketplace as a whole.

Bond: A loan that you have made to a company or government.

Whatever entity borrowed the money from you has to pay interest to you on the loan (a payment similar to a stock yield or dividend). Most importantly, the company or government can't change the amount or payment schedule of the interest it owes. Also, if the company goes bankrupt, and there is any money left over after the creditors have been paid off, bond holders get paid first before the stock holders.

Broker or Registered Representative: Brokers, more accurately called registered representatives, are financial professionals who are allowed to recommend, buy, and sell securities and mutual funds for clients.

Capital gains tax: A tax investors pay on the profits they've earned from the sale of stocks or other property, such as your house, which may have appreciated in value.

Certified Financial Planner: Well-trained and experienced financial advisors achieve CFP® certification which requires taking a series of rigorous courses on an array of financial topics and pass a day-long examination.

Charted Financial Analyst: A CFA candidate must have a college degree to be considered for the program. Then, they have to complete certification program training to develop expertise in financial and security analysis, economics, and investment management.

Chartered Financial Consultant: The ChFC or Chartered Financial Consultant certification requires the same core coursework as the CFP® certification, along with a few additional courses aimed at expanding the applicant's training in personal financial planning.[70]

Cognitive dissonance: A mental state in which the brain has two conflicting thoughts and tries to alleviate psychological stress by emphasizing the more positive or appealing one and de-emphasizing the other. When it comes to assessing our success in selecting investments, this kind of illusion can breed performance-killing overconfidence in our decision-making.

Corporate bond: A loan an investor makes to a corporation that the corporation then pays back with interest.

Defined Benefit Plan. A type of traditional pension whereby the employer funds your retirement by making donations to a retirement plan and when you retire, the plan pays you a monthly stipend, the amount of which is determined by your length of service and final pay.

Dividend: The amount a company pays its stock owners. The company has the right to raise, lower or eliminate a dividend.

Duration: The period of time over which a bond loan extends. The bond issuer pays the investor interest on the loan periodically throughout the duration. At the end of the duration, the bond issuer repays the loan's principle to the investor.

Elegantitis: A word I use to describe a disorder in which all current income is spent on goods and services of high-perceived value, such as imported luxury cars, large homes, vacation homes, expensive jewelry, country club membership and private schools. I've seen this disorder take root among friends, family, and colleagues, and my observation convinces me that elegantitis will keep you from retiring early.

Exchange Traded Fund (ETF): Mutual funds, including index funds, that trade like stocks.

Fiduciary: An advisor who must represent the best interests of the client. A fiduciary duty carries with it the advisor's ethical and legal responsibility to do the very best for the clients they represent.

Financial advisor: A person or group of investment experts contracted to help a client invest. The term encompasses a large group of people in the investment industry including those that are certified to those who have taken courses given by their investment companies and may actually be sales people.

Growth stock: A stock in a company in a rapid period of growth that does not pay dividends. All company profits are plowed back into the growth of the company. Investor profits are made by appreciation in the value of the company and increasing stock price. A growth stock may become a dividend paying stock as the company matures and growth rates moderate. Microsoft is a classic example.

Herd investing: Investing decisions based on perceptions of what "everyone else is doing" rather than on hard data.

Heuristics: General rules investors apply in their decision-making processes when they don't have a complete set of specific facts to guide them. When the problems we want to solve are complicated and shaped by a large number of variables and information points, like investment decisions, we may apply heuristics to very specific situations, so we can arrive at decisions quickly. While heuristics may represent "intelligent guess work," they're still guesses,

Income stock: A stock which kicks off a significant portion of its profits as cash to its stock holders. Utility companies such as Verizon and Duke Power pay significant dividends, as do real-estate investment trusts (REITS).

Index fund: A type of mutual fund in which a large group of stocks or bonds is collected and organized on the basis of individual value. The Dow Jones Index is ranked by stock price whereas the Standard and Poor's 500 Index is ranked by the value of the company.

Inertia and status quo: A behavioral bias that encourages investors to leave their money in current investments, even when the facts indicate those investments may not be the best choice.

Opportunity cost. Your second-best choice. It's the investment choice you did not choose because you spent $20,000 on snowmobiles. I will be talking a lot about opportunity cost in this book because it tends to be forgotten when you make a lousy investment.

Municipal bond: A loan an investor makes to a city, state, or other local government issuer that the issuer repays with interest.

Mutual Fund: A collection of stocks, bonds, real estate, precious metals, or even foreign currencies purchased by a large group of individual investors and managed by a central individual or organization.

Mutual fund load: This is a transactional fee, charged when an investor buys (a front-end load) or sells (a back-end load) shares in a mutual fund. Level-loaded Shares may not have an up-front load but have a yearly 12b-1 fee and an added fee if you sell the fund early. Loads basically are sales charges used to compensate a financial professional for advice.

Opportunity cost: The price you pay by not taking your second-best choice. A good example of opportunity cost is the difference between what you pay to send your child to private school vs. the tax you pay for your local schools or the price you paid to invest in your brother-in-law's carpet cleaning business vs. the S&P 500 index.

Principle: The amount of money investors contribute to their investments.

Registered Financial Consultant: Another registered type of financial advisor. To earn RFC certification, applicants must have any one of fifteen qualifying degrees or certifications, or complete an approved college curriculum. They also must meet the RFC licensing and experience requirements.

Registered Investment Advisor: An RIA can be either an individual or a firm that offers investment advice. To be certified as an RIA, applicants must take a qualifying examination and be registered with the SEC or with the state securities authorities.

Scams: Illegal schemes that unscrupulous individuals use to steal investors' money. The most common of these include *Ponzi schemes* in which a scam artist pays "dividends" to old investors using new investors' money; when the scheme runs out of new investors, the money flow stops and everyone (but the scam artist) loses; *pyramid schemes*, in which people are recruited as salespeople for a product or service, when in fact, the real goal of the operation is to collect the recruit's investment in fees for initial set-up and stocking, and then to encourage that person to recruit more people to similarly "invest"; *affinity schemes*, in which scammers target a specific group of people to invest in a bogus fund or stock; and, *pump and dump schemes*, in which one or more investors buy up numerous shares of a relatively worthless stock, hype the stock wildly to new investors, then sell off all of their shares when they've succeeded in driving up the stock's price—which tanks after the sell-off.

Stock or **equity**; You are a part owner in a company when you own its *stock*. The amount of stock you hold in a company represents your portion of that company's ownership. When you own shares of a company's stock your part ownership is called *equity*. It's like the equity you hold in your house; the part of the overall price that you've paid is your home equity.

Suitable investment advice: An investment standard by which an advisor is only obliged to recommend an investment that meets the client's needs, even if that investment isn't best alternative. This low-bar is the most current position of most current investment advisors.

Time horizon: The period over which an investment can be left to grow without being accessed by the investor. A *savings time horizon* usually extends three years or less. An *investment time horizon* may extend from three years to thirty years or more.

Treasury bond: A loan that an investor makes to the government that the government then repays with interest.

Value Stocks: Stocks that frequently kick off dividends which may actually be a relatively higher percentage of the stock price because the market place undervalues the company based on earning and sales or even plant and equipment.**Wrap fee:** The annual fee paid to a financial broker or advisor for a whole range of services, including advice, research, and more. The fee, which typically replaces front-end and back-end loads, may be 1.0% to 2% of the total amount of assets in the investment.

Yield: income you earn from your investment, such as interest or dividends. Yield is usually expressed as a percent.

[1] Roise, Stephen. "The Growing Size and Incomes of the Upper Middle Class," Urban Institute Report, June 21, 2016. http://www.urban.org/research.

[2] McCarthy, Kevin. "Just Over Half of Americans Own Stocks, Matching Record Low," Gallup Economy online, April 20, 2016. http://www.gallup.com/poll/190883/half-americans-own-stocks-matching-record-low.aspx

[3] Satovsky, Jonathan. "Smart People Can Make Stupid Investing Decisions," *Forbes* online, August 16, 2012. https://www.forbes.com/sites/greatspeculations/2012/08/16/smart-people-can-make-stupid-investing-decisions/#33b2fadf15d5

[4] Kahneman, Danile and Deaton, Angus. "High income improves evaluation of life but not emotional well-being."Center for Health and Well-being, Princeton University, Princeton, NJ 08544. Contributed August 4, 2010 (sent for review July 4, 2010).

[5] Kontis, Vasilis et al. "Future life expectancy in 35 industrialized countries: projections with a Bayesian model ensemble," The Lancet , Volume 389 , Issue 10076 , 1323 - 1335.

[6] Northwestern Mutual Life Insurance Company. "Welcome to the Longevity Game," The Northwestern Mutual Life Insurance Company, Milwaukee, WI. https://www.northwesternmutual.com/learning-center/tools/the-longevity-game.

[7] Chetty, J, stepner, M, Abraham S. "The Association Between Income and Life Expectancy in the United States, 2001-2014," JAMA:2016; 1750-1766.

[8] Vanguard online. "Vanguard: World's Largest Stock and Bond Funds Lower Expense Ratios," 27 April 2017. https://pressroom.vanguard.com/news/Press-Release-Vanguard-Expense-Ratio-April-2017.html

[9] Investopedia online. "Opportunity Cost." *Investopedia,* retrieved 8/3/2017. http://www.investopedia.com/terms/o/opportunitycost.asp

[10] Svenson, O *(1981). "Are We All Less Risky and More Skillful than Our Fellow Drivers?" Acta Psychologica 47 (1981) 143-148 0 North-Holland Publishing Company,* *https://pdfs.semanticscholar.org/ad37/e00352406dd776bc010769489b2412951c7d.pdf*

[11] Investopedia online, 6/23/2017. http://www.investopedia.com/terms/h/heuristics.asp#ixzz4ksB1ts97

[12] Edwards, Jim. *"One of the kings of the '90s dot-com bubble now faces 20 years in prison,"* Business Insider online, Dec. 6, 2016. http://www.businessinsider.com/where-are-the-kings-of-the-1990s-dot-com-bubble-bust-2016-12/#now-he-faces-20-years-in-prison-after-being-extradited-from-a-colombian-jail-2 (June 27, 2017)

[13] CNN Money. "10 big dot com flops: etoys," March 10, 2010. http://money.cnn.com/galleries/2010/technology/1003/gallery.dot_com_busts/3.html

[14] Value Penguin. "Average Bank Interest Rates in 2017: Checking, Savings, Money Market, and CD Rates."
https://www.valuepenguin.com/banking/average-bank-interest-rates
[15] Social Security Administration. Monthly Statistical Snapshot, May 2017.
https://www.ssa.gov/policy/docs/quickfacts/stat_snapshot/
[16] O'Connell, Brian. "The Mentality of Herd Investing," Prudential online. Prudential Financial, Inc.
https://www.prudential.com/personal/insights/investing-for-outcomes/herd-investing. Accessed 8/29/2017.
[17] Beattie, Andrew. "Market Crashes: The Tulip and Bulb Craze," *Investopedia*.
http://www.investopedia.com/features/crashes/crashes2.asp. Accessed August 29, 2017.
[18] Ibid.
[19] Brook, David. "The Mental Virtues." *New York Times,* August 28, 2014.
https://www.nytimes.com/2014/08/29/opinion/david-brooks-the-mental-virtues.html?_r=0
[20] Investopedia online. "Opportunity Cost." *Investopedia,* retrieved 8/3/2017.
http://www.investopedia.com/terms/o/opportunitycost.asp
[21] DQYDJ website, July 2, 2017. "Net Worth in the United States: Zooming in on the Top Centiles," https://dqydj.com/net-worth-in-the-united-states-zooming-in-on-the-top-centiles/ on July 7, 2017.
[22] U.S. Government Census Data,
https://www.census.gov/construction/nrs/pdf/uspricemon.pdf. Accessed February 15, 2018
[23] Powell, Farran. "10 Most, Least Expensive Private Colleges," *US News and World Report,* Sept. 13, 2016. https://www.usnews.com/education/best-colleges/the-short-list-college/articles/2016-09-13/10-most-least-expensive-private-colleges
[24] Rhee, Nari, PhD and Ilana Boivie. "The Continuing Retirement Savings Crisis." National Institute on Retirement Security, Washington D.C. March 2015. Available at
SSRN: https://ssrn.com/abstract=2785723 or http://dx.doi.org/10.2139/ssrn.2785723
[25] Ibid
[26] Proctor, Bernadette D.; Semega, Jessica L.; Kollar, Melissa A. "Income and Poverty in the United States: 2015," United States Census Bureau Report Number: P60-256. September 13, 2016.
https://www.census.gov/library/publications/2016/demo/p60-256.html
[27] The 2016 U.S. Trust Insights on Wealth and Worth®
[28] U.S. Department of Labor. "Consumer Expenditure Survey," Bureau of Labor Statistics. Annual and mid-year data reported on the BLS website at https://www.bls.gov/cex/.

[29] Morrell, Alex ; and Kiersz, Andy. "Seeing how the highest and lowest-earners spend their money will make you think differently about 'rich' vs. 'poor'" *Business Insider,* Mar. 26, 2017. http://www.businessinsider.com/how-high-income-and-low-income-americans-spend-their-money-2017-3

[30] United States Department of Agriculture Economic Research Service. "Food Prices and Spending," Economic Research Service using data from the U.S. Bureau of Labor Statistics. Updated April 25, 2017. https://www.ers.usda.gov/data-products/ag-and-food-statistics-charting-the-essentials/food-prices-and-spending/

[31] Ibid

[32] Ibid

[33] U.S. Department of Labor. "Consumer Expenditure Survey," Bureau of Labor Statistics. Annual and mid-year data reported on the BLS website at https://www.bls.gov/cex/.

[34] Ibid Morrell and Kiersz, 2017.

[35] Piersanti, Steve. "The Ten Awful Truths about Book Publishing," https://www.bkconnection.com/bkblog/steve-piersanti/the-10-awful-truths-about-book-publishing. Updated September 26, 2016.

[36] American Consumer Credit Council. "More than 90 Percent of Young Americans Would Loan Money to a Family Member in Need," ACCC online, November 14, 2013. http://www.consumercredit.com/about-us/press-releases/2013-press-releases/lending-money-to-family-and-friends-survey-results-consumercreditcom. Accessed 08/16/2017.

[37] Board of Governors of the Federal Reserve System. "Report on the Economic Well-Being of U.S. Households in 2014," Board of Governors of the Federal Reserve System Washington, DC 20551. May 2015. www.federalreserve.gov/publications/default.htm.

[38] Case Shiller Home Price Index. Accessed online August 11, 2017 at multpl.com. http://www.multpl.com/case-shiller-home-price-index-inflation-adjusted/

[39] You can find home mortgage and expense calculators at www.truehomecost.com, http://www.realtor.com/mortgage/tools/rent-or-buy-calculator/, and at www.zillow.com/mortgage-calculator. Freddie Mac offers a buy versus rent calculator at http://calculators.freddiemac.com/response/lf-freddiemac/calc/home10

[40] Darby, Mary. "In Ponzi We Trust," *Smithsonian Magazine* online, December 1998. http://www.smithsonianmag.com/history/in-ponzi-we-trust-64016168/. Accessed August 21, 2017.

[41] Grossman, Samantha. "Schemers and Swindlers: Charles Ponzi," Time online, Wednesday, Mar. 07, 2012. http://content.time.com/time/specials/packages/article/0,28804,2104982_2104983_2104997,00.html. Accessed August 21, 2017.

[42] Love, Bruce. "Investors beware: the Ponzi scheme is thriving," Financial Times online, March 29, 2017. https://www.ft.com/content/000a2dc6-e322-11e6-9645-c9357a75844a. Accessed August 21, 2017.

[43] The Wall Street Journal. "Madoff's Victims," The Wall Street Journal: US Edition. March 6, 2009. http://s.wsj.net/public/resources/documents/st_madoff_victims_20081215.html. Accessed August 21, 2017.

[44] U.S. Securities and Exchange Commission, "Investor Bulletin: Affinity Fraud." Investor.gov online, 09/26/2012. https://investor.gov/additional-resources/news-alerts/alerts-bulletins/investor-bulletin-affinity-fraud. Accessed August 22, 2017.

[45] Ibid

[46] Freddie Mac information editors. "3 Red Flags + 4 Tips to Fight Affinity Fraud," Freddie Mac online, http://www.freddiemac.com/singlefamily/news/2016/0428_affinity_fraud_sfnc.html. Accessed August 31, 2017.

[47] The Securities and Exchange Commission (SEC) is available online at www.sec.gov; by mail at Office of Investor Education and Advocacy, 100 F Street, NE, Washington, DC 20549-0213; Telephone: (800) 732-0330. The Financial Industry Regulatory Authority is available online at www.finra.org/investors; by mail at FINRA Complaints and Tips 9509 Key West Avenue, Rockville, MD 20850; Telephone: (301) 590-6500. You can contact your state securities regulator via the North American Securities Associates Administration online at www.nsaa.org.

[48] Cussen, Mark P., CFP®, CMFC, AFC. "CFP, CLU Or ChFC - Which Is Best?," Investopedia. http://www.investopedia.com/articles/professionaleducation/08/cfp-clu-chfc.asp, accessed August 29, 2017.

[49] The Financial Industry Regulatory Authority. "Choosing an Investment Professional: Brokers," FINRA online. http://www.finra.org/investors/brokers. Accessed August 30, 2017.

[50] Miller, Anna. "Outsmarting Con Artists," Monitor on Psychology, American Psychological Association online, http://www.apa.org/monitor/2013/02/con-artists.aspx. Accessed August 30, 2017.

[51] Financial Industry Regulatory Authority. "Avoiding Investment Scams," FINRA online, http://www.finra.org/investors/alerts/avoiding-investment-scams. Accessed August 30, 2017.

[52] Bernicke, Ty A. "The Real Cost of Owning a Mutual Fund," Forbes online, 4/04/2011, https://www.forbes.com/2011/04/04/real-cost-mutual-fund-taxes-fees-retirement-bernicke.html. Accessed 9/5/2017.

[53] Thune, Kent. "Average Expense Ratios for Mutual Funds," The Balance online, June 21, 2016. https://www.thebalance.com/average-expense-ratios-for-mutual-funds-2466612. Accessed 9/7/2017.

[54] http://www.finra.org/investors/alerts/class-b-mutual-fund-shares-do-they-make-grade Accessed September 27, 2017.

[55] Bell, Amy. "Understanding the New 'T' Shares. *Investopedia* online, April 29, 2017. http://www.investopedia.com/investing/understanding-new-t-shares/. Accessed September 12, 2017.

[56] https://www.slickcharts.com/sp500. Accessed February 19, 2018.

[57] McNabb, Bill. "Is Active Management Dead?", *Vanguard Blog for Investors,* January 10, 2017. https://vanguardadvisorsblog.com/2017/01/10/is-active-management-dead/. Accessed September 27, 2017.

[58] https://personal.vanguard.com/us/faces/JSP/Funds/Compare/CompareEntry Content.jsp Accessed February 22, 2018

[59] https://personal.vanguard.com/us/faces/JSP/Funds/Compare/CompareEntry Content.jsp Accessed February 25, 2018.

[60] Harbron, Garrett L., J.D., CFA, CFP®; Robers, Daren R.; and Rowley, James J. Jr., CFA. "The Case for Low-Cost Index-Fund Investing. *Vanguard Research,* April 2017. https://personal.vanguard.com/pdf/ISGIDX.pdf. Accessed September 27, 2017.

[61] Davis, Marc. "How September 11 Affected the U.S. Stock Market," *Investopedia* online, updated September 11, 2017. http://www.investopedia.com/financial-edge/0911/how-september-11-affected-the-u.s.-stock-market.aspx. Accessed September 14, 2017.

[62] Ibid.

[63] Fidelity® 500 Index Fund - Institutional Premium Class FXAIX. Fidelity.com

[64] Dalbar. "Quantitative Analysis of Investor Behavior, 2016," DALBAR, Inc. www.dalbar.com. DALBAR, Inc. 303 Congress Street Boston, MA 02210 . Accessed September 17, 2017.

[65] Ibid.

[66] Pfau, Wade D. "A Warning to the Advisory Profession: DALBAR's Math is Wrong."*Advisor Perspectives,* March 6, 2017. https://www.advisorperspectives.com/articles/2017/03/06/a-warning-to-the-advisory-profession-dalbar-s-math-is-wrong. Accessed September 27, 2017.

[67] Morningstar Risk Tolerance Questionnaire, https://corporate.morningstar.com/us/documents/NASDCompliance/IWT_Curr entReport_RiskToleranceQuest.pdf; Vanguard Investor Questionnaire, https://personal.vanguard.com/us/FundsInvQuestionnaire; Rutgers Investment Risk Tolerance Quiz, https://njaes.rutgers.edu/money/riskquiz/. All accessed September 19, 2017.

[68] Kitces, Michael. "The Sorry State of Risk Tolerance Questionnaires for Financial Advisors," *Nerd's Eye View at Kitces.com,* September 14, 2016. https://www.kitces.com/blog/risk-tolerance-questionnaire-and-risk-profiling-problems-for-financial-advisors-planplus-study/. Accessed September 19, 2017.

[69] Kosnett, Jeffrey and Landis, David. "Tax-Free Bonds," *Kiplinger,* February 28, 2008. http://www.kiplinger.com/article/investing/T052-C000-S002-tax-free-bonds.html. Accessed September 19, 2017.

[70] Cussen, Mark P., CFP®, CMFC, AFC. "CFP, CLU Or ChFC - Which Is Best?," Investopedia. http://www.investopedia.com/articles/professionaleducation/08/cfp-clu-chfc.asp, accessed August 29, 2017.

ABOUT THE AUTHOR

Lyle Victor writes about his two great passions; medicine and economics. His first four efforts were text books on critical care and pulmonary medicine and a handbook for medical trainee workplace and financial survival. Get Rich by Saying NO! is a product of seminars he has given on investing to medical students, residents and colleagues and of decades of learning from his mistakes and those of his colleagues, friends and family. Dr. Victor received his MD degree from the Icahn School of Medicine at Mount Sinai and a MBA from the University of Michigan, Ross School of Business

95891634R00131